WHY
DIDN'T THEY TELL ME?

Also by Morris Venden

Wonderful Words of Life
95 Theses on Righteousness by Faith
The Answer Is Prayer
Faith That Works
God Says, but I Think
Hard to Be Lost
Here I Come, Ready or Not
How Jesus Treated People
How to Know God's Will in Your Life
Love God and Do As You Please
Modern Parables
Morning Manna
Never Without an Intercessor
Nothing to Fear
To Know God
Your Friend, the Holy Spirit

MORRIS VENDEN

SHARING JESUS ISN'T SOMETHING WE DO. IT'S WHO WE ARE.

WHY
DIDN'T THEY TELL ME?

Pacific Press® Publishing Association
Nampa, Idaho
Oshawa, Ontario, Canada
www.pacificpress.com

Book design by Eucaris L. Galicia
Cover photo/illustration © PunchStock.com

Texts credited to the NIV are from the Holy Bible, New International Version.
Copyright © 1973, 1978, 1984 by the International Bible Society.
Used by permission of Zondervan Bible Publishers.

Library of Congress Cataloging-in-Publication Data

Venden, Morris L.
Why didn't they tell me? : sharing Jesus isn't something we do,
it's who we are / Morris Venden.
p.cm.
ISBN 0-8163-2080-2
1. Witness bearing (Christianity) 2. Seventh-day Adventists—Doctrines. I. Title.

BV4520.V45 2005
248'.5—dc22   2004065495

Additional copies of this book are available by calling toll free 1-800-765-6955 or
by visiting http://www.adventistbookcenter.com.

05 06 07 08 09 • 5 4 3 2 1

DEDICATION

To my wife who has stayed with me and supported me through the joys and sorrows, ups and downs of over fifty years of ministry. She encouraged me to keep going when I wanted to quit. Eternal gratitude to Mary Lou.

CONTENTS

Foreword 8

1. Finishing the Work in China 11

2. Working Out Your Own Salvation 27

3. The Work of the Holy Spirit 38

4. Lions in the Street 50

5. Fishing on the Right Side 62

6. Holy Sweat 76

7. Intercessory Prayer 85

8. The Least of These 94

9. The Woman at the Well, Part I 106

10. The Woman at the Well, Part II 117

FOREWORD

It would be accurate to say that Jesus was controversial. He didn't set out to be. He just told the truth about God and the kingdom of heaven, and many (especially leaders) were offended by what He had to say.

Why Didn't They Tell Me? has the potential to have a similar effect for similar reasons. For too long, we have been conditioned to think of the Christian witness as dispensing information rather than as sharing a personal experience. We have talked about "the truth" as though it were a set of fundamental beliefs, but according to Jesus, the "Truth" is a Person. *He* is the Truth! Knowing the "Truth" is really about knowing the Lord! When we know Him as our personal Friend, our witness changes from merely being logically persuasive to being overwhelmingly contagious.

If Scripture is clear about anything, it is clear that God is out looking for friends. Amazing though it may seem, Heaven is hungry for friendship. All the leaves of Scripture are rustling with an invitation to a personal relationship with God. Those who respond to that invitation, have something to share that the whole world is searching for.

Jesus didn't restrict the Great Commission to a handful of super-salesmen evangelists. He didn't ask the clergy to assume responsibility for getting the work done. He asked *every* believer to tell what they know about *Him*.

People are not waiting to hear professional proclamations. They are waiting to hear what we ourselves have seen and heard and felt of the power of Christ. This is the witness for which our Lord calls, and for want of which the world is perishing.

Some will think this book has it all wrong and that it flies in the face of evangelism. But for those who have ears to hear, it will strike a chord of response and launch a symphony of praise.

Why Didn't They Tell Me? will make *you* want to tell *them!*

Thanks, Dad, for yet another book which reminds us that it really is all about Him!

Lee Venden
College Place, Washington

CHAPTER 1

FINISHING THE WORK IN CHINA

A Chinese college professor had a beautiful, brilliant daughter. He was interested in making sure she got the best husband. He had a difficult time accomplishing this task because there was just no one good enough for her, so he came up with a plan. He would put on a billboard, in the middle of town, one hundred of the most obscure and dimly understood Chinese characters, and the man who could understand the most of these characters would have his daughter in marriage.

A number of suitors tried, and the most any of them got was 80 percent. The professor was not satisfied. He wanted 100 percent.

One day a cobbler came to town and saw the billboard. He looked at it and said, "What a pity. I don't know one." And the townspeople said, "That's the closest anyone has come yet. He knows all of them except one." They went and told the professor, and the cobbler got the daughter in marriage.

On the wedding night she asked him which character he didn't know. He said, "You don't understand. I didn't know any of them." This got back to the emperor, who called him in and said, "No one in my kingdom is going to treat my subjects this way. I'm going to ask you three questions, and if you can't answer them, it's your head." He continued, "The questions are going to be with hand motions. No talking. I make a motion, and you answer with hand motion."

The emperor started by drawing circles in the air with his pointer finger. The cobbler motioned back by holding one hand up next to his shoulders and the other by his waist with the palms facing each other. The emperor was pleased as he wanted to know what to do with the enemies that surrounded him. And he understood the cobbler to say, "Suppress them."

Then the emperor held up three fingers. The cobbler, beginning from the waist and going down, swung his arms back with his palms open backwards. The emperor was pleased. As he motioned he had asked, "What do I do with the three enemies that are the most terrible of all the enemies?" And he understood the cobbler to say, "Don't worry about them."

For the last question the emperor moved his hand first pointing up and then down. In answer, the cobbler smiled and patted his hip. The emperor was again pleased. With his gesture he had asked the cobbler, "What do I do about the two worst enemies above and below?" And he understood the cobbler to say, "Sit on your throne and don't worry." So he sent the cobbler back to the beautiful daughter.

On their honeymoon, the daughter asked the cobbler how things went with the emperor. He said, "Great! The emperor asked me how many pancakes I can eat. I said, 'A stack that high.' He asked, 'Can't you eat three more?' I said, 'No way!' Then he asked, 'Where should you get the leather for your shoe business, from the upper part of the body, or from below?' I said, 'From the hip of the animal.' "

In this Chinese fable, we have an example of miscommunication.

I took a trip to China a few years back that had a tremendous impact on me. It reminded me of the miscommunication we have concerning God, His character, His work, and the people He has created. There is no place like China to remind you of this. In the first place, China is a country geographically about the size of the United States and it has five times the population—about 1.3 billion people. Talk about crowds. As one person said to me, if you were walking downtown in Shanghai and you fainted, you wouldn't even fall down for three blocks. The crowds are ominous.

Some years ago the church leadership in North America asked pastors to divide up the territory around them and plan strategies to reach the people of the world with the gospel. I didn't think of the crowds then. I was pastor of the church at Pacific Union College, in a predominantly Seventh-day Adventist community. We, the pastoral staff, laughed and said, "We have forty people on Howell Mountain who are not of our faith, and we have two thousand church members. No problem!"

Another time I found myself in Bombay, India, with millions of people, many of them sleeping on the streets and people walking over them at night—father, mother, children, grandparents, dog, cat. And the church in Bombay, India, with eighty members, was supposed to reach them all. How is that going to happen?

Then you put your foot in China, with 1.3 billion people, and you say, "And we have been trying to do the Lord's work!" That's our problem. *We* have been trying to do the *Lord's* work. It's about time we stopped trying to do the *Lord's* work.

Where does the miscommunication come in? The main passage of Scripture used for years to get the church off the dime and busy working is found in Ezekiel.

" 'When I say to the wicked, "O wicked man, you will surely die," and you do not speak out to dissuade him from his ways, that wicked man will die for his sin, and I will hold you accountable for his blood. But if you do warn the wicked man to turn from his ways and he does not do so, he will die for his sin, but you will have saved yourself' " (Ezekiel 33:8, 9).

I have grown up with this idea, and it used to coerce me into witness and service. The assumption is that I am the watchman in this verse, and that the wicked is the great world out there, including 1.3 billion in China.

Big miscommunication!

As a result of this approach, we have people who are frightened of witness and service because if someone is going to live or die based upon my witness and my success or failure in it, then I don't want to get involved. I will get the professionals to do the job, and I will pay them the money. With this approach, we have killed the Christian witness in the church. Who wants to suffer the guilt that would come from thinking that I might have failed when I could have hired the satellite program speaker to do the job?

Another result of this thinking is that it has brought the character of God into ill repute. God, who is the Author of life and who knows we had no choice in being born into this world, would not be a God of love if He left someone's eternal destiny on the shoulders of some other person. This also brings into ill repute the character of God in terms of His power. Isn't He big enough to do the job? Why does He lay it on us?

A little book called *Steps to Christ* says, "God might have committed the message of the gospel, and all the work of loving ministry, to the heavenly angels. He might have employed other means for accomplishing His purpose" (79). Many times I've asked myself, why didn't He? The angels wouldn't goof like I do and turn someone away by a wrong word or look. So, there have been many, many misunderstandings and miscommunications concerning the mission and the purpose of the church and Christian witness and service because of one passage of Scripture from which we glean the wrong information.

Augustine came along with his doctrine of original sin, which says that we are born sinners and we are *accountable* for it. When you are quoting the doctrine of original sin as expressed by Augustine, you are including the idea of "I am at fault, I am to blame, I am responsible, I am accountable for being born in the world of sin." The things that follow, of course, are very common in the Catholic Church today—infant baptism and other things relating to the idea that we must get this problem taken care of early because we are accountable. Coupled with that is the passage in Ezekiel that makes me think I am accountable and my blood will be required if so-and-so is lost and I did not try to save him.

Another thing that comes to mind when one travels to these densely populated countries is the realization that people are still being born faster than the entire Christian church is taking the gospel to them, let alone the three angels' messages. I heard someone trying to explain how that's not true, but I don't know what kind of stretch of imagination or what kind of a calculator they were using. Even with the birth control that is required in China, around the world people are still being born faster than we are taking the gospel to them.

Here is another question: If a person's eternal destiny is based upon what we do, why should anyone ever hear the gospel twice before everyone has heard the gospel once? Yet we go over the same territories again and again. We like to go into places where people are responding and hundreds are being baptized. We don't like it as well to go into places like the Middle East, where very few are interested. In our humdrum activities and our feverish attempts to try and cause church growth, we need to put a foot inside China and realize that we are not going to finish anything.

There are possibly eighty million Christians in China under the Three Self movement, a movement led by David Lamb, and it is under him that our own churches operate. While I was in China, our visiting group met with the Adventist believers in Beijing, more than a thousand members who meet in a building that is not their own—it is owned and run by the government under the Three Self program of all Christians in China. Then we met with people at the Adventist hospital, Sir Run Run Shaw Hospital. We got a little glimpse of what is going on there. I began to realize that unless God finishes His work, we're all dead.

In Acts 17 Paul was burdened with the Greeks he met at Mars' Hill, where he said some very significant things.

" 'The God who made the world and everything in it is the Lord of heaven and earth and does not live in temples built by hands. And he is not served by human hands, as if he needed anything, because he himself gives all men life and breath and everything else' " (Acts 17:24, 25).

This is very interesting as we think of all the churches today. God does not live in temples built by hands. But the temples to other gods in our world today are numerous. Of course, in China the temples are everywhere—to Buddha and other gods. I got depressed after we visited so many temples. How can they worship and bow down to this fat, laughing, smiling Buddha? Have you seen him? *It's laughable that they would do that,* I thought. And in my depression, as I watched this, I began to wonder if it's just a matter of perspective.

I remembered the story about the Americans in Japan who made fun of Japanese religion. They were bold enough to make fun of the Japanese who put food out for their dead loved ones at the graves, and they asked the Japanese, "When are your loved ones going to come up and eat the food?" The Japanese replied, "At the same time that yours come up to smell the flowers." Maybe it is just a matter of perspective. When I go to a Buddhist temple and I'm turned off by it, I wonder what they would think if they went to the garden at Jerusalem and saw a dirty, empty tomb. Would they be any more impressed? So I began to think, is it just a matter of perspective?

Then I go to the Word of God, which we understand is the basis of everything. It says,

> " 'From one man he made every nation of men, that they should inhabit the whole earth; and he determined the times set for them and the exact places where they should live. God did this so that men would seek him and perhaps reach out for him and find him, though he is not far from each one of us. "For in him we live and move and have our being" . . . "We are his offspring." Therefore since we are God's offspring, we should not think that the divine being is like gold or silver or stone—an image made by man's design and skill. In the past God overlooked such ignorance, but now he commands all people everywhere to repent' " (Acts 17:26–30).

As we study further we discover, in the two verses just before this speech, an interesting statement:

"Paul then stood up in the meeting of the Areopagus and said: 'Men of Athens! I see that in every way you are very religious. For as I walked around and looked carefully at your objects of worship, I even found an altar with this inscription: TO AN UNKNOWN GOD. Now what you worship as something unknown I am going to proclaim to you' " (Acts 17:22, 23).

It suddenly dawned on me that he didn't say, "You're worshipping the wrong god." What he said was, "You're worshipping God, but you are ignorant about the God you are worshipping."

Is there a difference? Is it possible that people in other countries of other religions can worship God by another name? Or is that too scary for a Christian to consider? Is it possible that God is fair enough and loving enough and logical enough to admit that if He is a God of love, that He is responsible for us living and moving and having our being and not we ourselves? (See Acts 17:28.) Is it possible that He, in order to continue to be a God of love, would have to give everyone born in this world an adequate opportunity for something better, regardless of what we do? Is it possible that He would not be a God of love, and it would bring into question His character, if He left the salvation of others dependent upon us, on what we do, and on whether the church succeeds or fails?

As I looked at the masses of people in China, I began to come up with this solid idea that God must have millions of people who could be worshipping Him ignorantly. Is that possible? They are worshipping according to the light they have, be it little or small, and no one is going to be lost because of what we do or don't do in the Christian church, except maybe for us. Is anyone going to be lost if I don't share, give, witness, and serve? Yes, I would be the one lost.

Because of the miscommunication created by using texts like the one in Ezekiel to prove that people's blood will be on our hands, we have parents who will lie awake at night with guilt and remorse concerning their own children. There were several on our trip who talked about it. They shared that half of their kids were in the faith and half have left the faith. I reminded them that God lost one-third of His kids. And just by way of comfort for your kids, the story isn't over yet. You mean God will give my children an adequate opportunity for salvation, whether I succeed or fail? Yes. God will give everyone in this world, with capacity, an adequate opportunity for salvation regardless of what we do. Otherwise He would not be a God of love, because I had no choice being born here in the first place.

Many years ago I heard Pastor H. M. S. Richards, Sr., talk at the Gladstone camp meeting in Oregon. He pointed out that regardless of what we think, most of God's children are out *there* in the world. Then he said, "You may think I'm wrong. But I'm right anyhow." It so happened that he was quoting a lady who had written a lot of books. So also you may think that I'm wrong on the premise that I'm taking in this book. But I'm right anyhow. And I believe that all you need to do to convince yourself that I'm right anyhow is to step your foot inside China.

Another old wives' tale that has been around a long time in the church is that children who have not reached the age of accountability will be saved or lost depending on what their parents do. So, up until the age of twelve, and we usually give that as the age, their eternal destiny will be decided by their parents.

This idea was exploded a long time ago. If you want to check it out, read *Selected Messages,* Book 2, page 260: "As the little infants come forth immortal from their dusty beds, they immediately wing their way to their mother's arms. They meet again nevermore to part. But many of the little ones have no mother there. We listen in vain for the rapturous song of triumph from the mother. The angels receive the motherless infants and conduct them to the tree of life." There will be babies in heaven with no parent because God cares about everyone He created. And He is no respecter of persons. This observation made in *Selected Messages* is based solidly on Scripture—Ezekiel 18:20: "The soul who sins is the one who will die. The son will not share the guilt of the father, nor will the father share the guilt of the son."

This brings us to the hope and the light that shines ever brighter as the world grows larger. It is found in John, who declared Jesus to be "the true light that gives light to every man [who] was com-

19

ing into the world" (John 1:9). You mean they have all heard of Christ? No, not necessarily. But He is still that light that lights everyone who comes into the world.

What about Acts 4:12, which says, "Salvation is found in no one else, for there is no other name under heaven given to men by which we must be saved"? In the name of Jesus, that's true. It's only because of Jesus that anyone is saved. As believers we know that. But the others may not know that until later. And the premise emerges that everyone born in this world will be given, sometime during their lives, an adequate opportunity to choose whether or not they're going to be lost.

This brings up an interesting switch. For a long time the evangelical world has held on to this old approach—that everyone is born lost in this world until they choose to be saved. That was based upon Augustinian theology and the idea of original sin. Along came an author by the name of Neal Punt not too long ago, who took the exact opposite view. He said that everyone in this world is born saved until they choose to be lost.

So the people in the world are not born sinners? Yes, they are born sinners. But we are not held accountable for it, because God has never held it against us that we were born on the wrong planet. Here are some verses to study: "Jesus said, 'For judgment I have come into this world, so that the blind will see and those who see will become blind.' " Then He added, " 'If you were blind, you would not be guilty of sin; but now that you claim you can see, your guilt remains' " (John 9:39–41).

Here's another one.

" 'If I had not come and spoken to them, they would not be guilty of sin. Now, however, they have no excuse for their sin. . . . If I had not done among them what no one else did, they would not be guilty of sin. But now they have seen these miracles, and yet they have hated both me and my Father' " (John 15:22–25).

What about this?

"(Indeed, when Gentiles, who do not have the law, do by nature things required by the law, they are a law for themselves, even though they do not have the law, since they show that the requirements of the law are written on their hearts, their consciences also bearing witness, and their thoughts now accusing, now even defending them.) This will take place on the day when God will judge men's secrets through Jesus Christ, as my gospel declares" (Romans 2:14–16).

And finally this one: "Anyone, then, who knows the good he ought to do and doesn't do it, sins" (James 4:17). Thus, Christ is the light that lights everyone who comes into the world, and until we understand light we are not held responsible. At whatever point we are given a revelation of light, be it big or small, and then we make a decision to go against it, at that point we choose to be lost.

When I read Punt, I thought, *I've read that somewhere before.* Suddenly I knew where. It was in the writings of the lady who wrote all the books. Let's look at some of these quotations.

" 'For the grace of God that bringeth salvation hath appeared to all men' " (*The Acts of the Apostles,* 205). Does that mean everyone who's ever been born in the world already? Yes. Here is another one: "The Spirit of God is freely bestowed to enable every man to lay hold upon the means of salvation. Thus Christ, 'the true light,' 'lighteth every man that cometh into the world.' John 1:9. Men fail of salvation only through their own willful refusal of the gift of life" (*The Great Controversy,* 262). So we are born sinners, but we are not held accountable until we understand truth. And at that point, we decide whether or not we're going to be lost.

But angels of heaven are passing throughout the length and breadth of the earth, seeking to comfort the sorrowing, to protect the imperiled, to win the hearts of men to Christ. Not one is neglected or passed by. [Not one.] God is no respecter of persons, and He has an equal care for all the souls He has created (*The Desire of Ages,* 639).

Isn't that good news? This one will blow you over.

Those whom Christ commends in the judgment may have known little of theology, but they have cherished His principles. . . . Among the heathen are those who worship God ignorantly [What are you doing bowing down to that fat, laughing Buddha? Doing it ignorantly.], those to whom the light is never brought by human instrumentality, yet they will not perish. Though ignorant of the written law of God, they have heard His voice speaking to them in nature, and have done the things that the law required. Their works are evidence that the Holy Spirit has touched their hearts, and they are recognized as the children of God.

How surprised and gladdened will be the lowly among the nations, and among the heathen, to hear from the lips of the Saviour, "Inasmuch as ye have done it unto one of the least of these My brethren, ye have done it unto Me"! How glad will be the heart of Infinite Love as His followers look up with surprise and joy at His words of approval! (*The Desire of Ages,* 638).

His followers? Yes, the ignorant, who have worshiped God ignorantly, who never saw the light from human instrumentalities. We used to sing a song, which even Tennessee Ernie Ford sang with gusto:

"Brightly beams our Father's mercy from His lighthouse evermore,

But to us He gives the keeping of the lights along the shore."

But then we begin to concentrate on the lights along the shore. We get to the chorus and become "me"-centered. We sing,

"Let the lower lights be burning; Send a gleam across the wave.

Some poor fainting, struggling seaman You may rescue, you may save" ("Brightly Beams Our Father's Mercy," Philip P. Bliss).

We concentrate on the lower lights and forget that *we* are the lower lights and that the bright beams are our *Father's* mercy shining from *His* lighthouse evermore.

We have noticed already that the Spirit is involved, and we have noticed that the angels are involved, and that we are just a drop in the bucket. We are not going to finish anything. If God doesn't finish it, nothing will get finished. All we have to do is look into the heavily populated countries and you will know that is true. And yet we have enough denominational ego to think that we are totally responsible.

Well, you say, what about those hard texts like Ezekiel? Check out the context, and it's pretty simple. It was revealed to Ezekiel. He was called the son of man, and the scripture we began with was talking about Ezekiel and his mission to Israel. It wasn't talking about your and my mission to the lost in the world or in China. Then someone is always going to bring along some rare unpublished quotation about Christless graves and millions lost. But if you check it out you'll find that a Christless grave is not necessarily a lost grave. And a lost person can be found.

While I visited China, I left some of my shirts hanging in the closet in Hong Kong. In the pocket of a shirt I left my credit cards and my driver's license. I managed to make a phone call back to the hotel and was thrilled when they informed me that my shirts and all their contents were found. What was lost was found. Jesus talked about the lost son and the lost coin and the lost sheep. But they were all found. God is committed to finding the lost, whether we are or not.

Salvation can be compared to walking from Los Angeles to Loma Linda, the "promised land." As I'm walking you come along in your car and you say, "Where are you going?"

"I'm going to Loma Linda, the promised land."

You say, "Get in. I'll take you there." So you have a part in my getting there, because you help me get there faster, and you probably even save me some blisters along the road. Yes, there are all kinds of differences that we can make, as Christians and as a church, in helping people along the road. And God might be able to use me to turn someone from going to Las Vegas, the "other place," and head them to Loma Linda. But if I don't do it, someone else will. And if I goof up in trying to save my children for the kingdom of heaven, God will give them another chance from many other sources. Therefore parents don't have to lie awake with guilt, thinking and wondering if they did it all wrong, because God is bigger than that. If you'll take the time to sit down with the book *Steps to Christ* and read the chapter on witnessing, you'll find out that the only reason God gave us a part to act in the plan of redemption is for our good.

Then what happens to the good that could come to me if all I do is pay a dollar to the satellite programs? Let's keep the satellite programs going but never as a substitute for the good God intended it to do for me. What good does it do for me if God gave me a part to act in the plan of redemption, and instead I give a dollar to the Voice of Prophecy or a dollar to It Is Written, or whatever, and I think that's going to do it?

We have gotten spooked by the idea that *we* are going to fail and cause someone to be lost. We have developed our stars, our center-stage people, who are doing the work for us, and we are giving them the money to do the work for us. Then we call that soul winning, when the truth is, church growth is not growth in membership. It is growth in the members. If the members will get involved in Christian witness and service, they will grow. And if they grow, the membership will grow. That is guaranteed.

As I contemplated putting a book together on this subject, I thought it would probably be the last book I write just before I'm excommunicated. But, please, neighbor, think. The title of this book came to me while I was in China: *Why Didn't They Tell Me?* Why didn't they tell me? I'm glad that we can be lower lights and that we can burn. But I'm much more thankful about His lighthouse ever more—Jesus, the light that lights everyone who comes into the world. Why would we want the whole responsibility to fall upon us? Can we be that naive? Can we be that unthinking? Can we be that foolish?

If this causes you to stop giving a dollar to the Voice of Prophecy and to stop being involved in Christian service and witness, then you've missed the point. If you read that chapter in *Steps to Christ*, you will discover the real reason why we witness and why we go. If we have tasted and seen that the Lord is good, we shall have something to say concerning our best Friend. Not just a dollar for the satellite programs but rather something to say concerning our best Friend. If we have tasted and seen that the Lord is good, we will not be able to hold our peace. The genuine Christian doesn't have to be coerced into witness and service by some kind of jolt maneuvers. The genuine Christian witnesses spontaneously. And the one who has a relationship with the best Friend they've ever had or known cannot keep quiet. It's about time we realize that this is the basis of genuine witness and service.

I don't want to sound angry. But I was angry when this began to dawn on me and I realized what a bill of goods had been sold to me by home, church, and school. I wish somewhere, sometime, someone would shout it from the housetops, the right approach to witness and service, so that we can really become involved with freedom and without worrying that our mistakes are going to cause someone to be lost.

I'm glad God is no respecter of persons. He has an equal regard for all the souls He has created, including the beggars who come along by the bus asking for money, the armless and the legless, the orphans. He has equal regard for the little seven-month-old baby that was sitting across the aisle from us on the airplane on our way back from China, who had been abandoned at a Chinese university, and someone from America paid twenty thousand dollars to take it home. God has an equal care for all the souls He has created. And that includes you.

CHAPTER 2

WORKING OUT YOUR OWN SALVATION

The next time you go to church, ask yourself these questions: Why did I come to church today? What is church all about anyway? In this chapter we will try to get a little better grasp on what church is all about.

Why church? We all know that it is a custom to go to church and that this custom has been around for a long time. But what is the reason for the existence of the church? Why are we here, as a church? What is our mission?

The church can be defined in at least three ways. The first is found in Acts 17:24, which shows the church as the brick, the mortar, the shingles, the chandeliers, the carpet and pews. This may not mean a whole lot at first glance, but look at this verse closely: " 'The God who made the world and everything in it is the Lord of heaven and earth and does not live in temples built by hands.' " This could be a slap in the face of one who places a lot of value in church buildings and huge cathedrals. But as the songwriter suggests, whether the building is a temple or a stable, it really doesn't matter as long as God is there and people who care are there.

It seems that the brick-and-mortar building, the edifice, isn't really that important, but Acts 17:24 isn't the only text that refers to church as a building. In John 2, Jesus made it clear during His cleansing of the temple that this was His Father's house. He said, " 'How dare you turn my Father's house into a market!' " (John 2:16). Jesus placed great value on the temple—the building, the stone, the brick and mortar—because it is His Father's house. And of course we dedicate buildings to God today.

Sometimes people get nervous about the amount of money that goes into a great new church, a big or fancy church building. We forget that the sanctuary in the wilderness represented a great deal of expense. Solomon's temple, which God blessed, represented far more than what people themselves lived in. Maybe that is a good rule of thumb. It's not wrong at all to have God's house at least be better than the house we live in. Why not even have a lavish house for God? Nothing is too good for God. But I suppose we can debate that for a long time in the physical realm.

Let's go on to the second definition of the church, which we call the organic church, or the organized church. The Bible speaks about the organic church in more ways than one. The apostle Paul wrote about the collection of churches he visited. We might even call it a denomination today. They were a group of churches with their headquarters in Jerusalem—an organized church. Organization had its place then; it always has and still does.

Jesus made it clear in His own book (Revelation is the only book that is Jesus' own book) that there is an organic church. The first three chapters of Revelation describe the local congregations in those days, and, also, the congregations are represented as churches in periods of history, apparently, to the close of time. Jesus would have to be talking about an organic church when He says that the church claims it is rich, increased with goods, and has need of nothing. He called it Laodicea, the lukewarm church. It would have to be an organized church because if it were what some people call the universal church—dedicated, committed, focused followers of Christ everywhere—it couldn't be lukewarm. So this passage is talking about a denomination, a congregation of people who have somehow lost their vision, their goal, and their God.

The organic church has its place, but there are people everywhere disenchanted with the organic church. They are too familiar with it. There are people living in your neighborhood who wouldn't go near an organic church, and there are people in my subculture of Seventh-day Adventists who are so disenchanted with the organic church that they couldn't care less about it anymore.

The organic church has done a lot of damage to the name of God. It has brought blame to God through its own image for a lot more than He deserves. I was watching a religious station on television one day, and I saw someone giving a report about a hundred million unchurched people in the United States, most of whom still care about God. What a challenge to the sincere followers of Christ!

The third type of church is the mystical church. Some people call it the universal church or the universal body of Christ. Many people, because of their disenchantment with the organic church, have a strong commitment to the mystical church. They say things like, "I don't have my name in any church book," or "I don't belong to any church membership list." What they mean is, "I'm beyond that," "I'm above that," or "That's below me." "I believe in the mystical body of Christ, people whose names are written only in heaven, and I'm not going to get involved in anything other than that. I'm through playing church. I'm going to belong to the mystical church." The implication is that this is the mature thing to do.

We might find some Bible evidence for the mystical church, but it is more difficult to find than for the building church and the organic church. I challenge you to find solid biblical evidence to any great extent suggesting that the church is only mystical or only universal, with names written only in heaven.

Jesus challenged this thought when He said, "I have other sheep that are not of this sheep pen" (John 10:16). If He was talking only about a universal mystical church, He couldn't be talking about other sheep not of this fold. Perhaps this refers to the world's religions, but would that answer the challenge? Evidently Jesus placed value upon the organic church and would like to have people aware that the church is the genuine fold.

Another evidence that Jesus placed a great deal of value upon the church other than simply the mystical one is Matthew 18:17. Jesus said that if you have a dispute with someone and they won't listen, take it to the church. If He were speaking of a mystical universal church, how would you know where to take the problem? If someone is going through a difficult time concerning their understanding of God and faith and church, Jesus made it clear that we should appeal to the church, which would have to be an organization.

Paul writes to Timothy about the leaders of the church. If the church was only mystical and universal, and no one could perceive where it is and who the members are, then how could it have leaders? What would be the purpose of the leadership, and of Paul telling them what kind of leaders they should be?

Apparently God has a purpose for church organization, which is able to do things that the individual cannot. Could you send a missionary to some foreign field all by yourself? Is there a family that has built a hospital all by themselves? Do you know of a person who has built a school all alone? Is there any individual in the mystical body of Christ who has ever been able to do what only the body of Christ—organized, planning, and strategizing—can do together? Do we really need to fault what has been done by organizations in spreading the gospel to all the world? Is it not a thrill to be able to travel to most any place in the world and realize that you will find evidence of the organic body of Christ at work?

So what is the purpose of the church? Is the primary purpose attendance? We like it when people attend the church, particularly if we have something to do with the leadership of the church. But is simply attending church where it's all at? Is attendance important as far as God is concerned? Paul makes it clear in the book of Hebrews, "Let us hold unswervingly to the hope we profess, for he who promised is faithful. And let us consider how we may spur one another on toward love and good deeds" (Hebrews 10:23, 24). The King James Version says "provoke unto love and to good works." And he adds, "Let us not give up meeting together, as some are in the habit of doing, but let us encourage one another— and all the more as you see the Day approaching" (Hebrews 10:25). God's idea is that we should not forsake meeting together. This is as biblical as you can get.

Some people say that if they go to church and make sure that they have their names written in the church books, this will guarantee them a place in the kingdom of heaven. Maybe you are not naive enough to actually say that, but it shows up in other ways, sometimes subtle, sometime not so subtle. There are people who, because of difficulties, find themselves outside the church, and they will not rest until they get their names on the church books again. They have the idea that it guarantees their eternal destiny.

Jesus had something to say about that. "Rejoice because your names are written in heaven" (Luke 10:20, NKJV). Having my name on the church books isn't going to mean a whole lot if my name isn't written in heaven. People whose names are written in heaven find it meaningful to be a part of the body of Christ by having their names written in the church books as well.

If I were interested in having my name in the church books only, I might find myself among the immature group of Christians interested only in getting instead of giving. The person who attends church may not always be able to get. The primary purpose for attending church is to give, not to get.

Probably our greatest example of someone who didn't get a whole lot from going to church is Jesus Himself. What did Jesus get when He went to church? He got led out of the church afterward to the edge of a cliff, where the members tried to throw Him off. If anyone had a good excuse to stay home and read His *Adventist Review,* it would have been Jesus. But "on the Sabbath day he went into the synagogue, as was his custom" (Luke 4:16). Is it good to go to church just out of custom? Evidently it's not all bad. Jesus did, and He went to church to give.

You may ask, What can I give when I go to church? I'm not the preacher. I'm not the Sabbath School teacher. I'm not one of the church leaders. One of the things we can give is praise to God. Praise to God coming from a sincere heart means something to Him. That's why He created us with the power of choice in the first place. We know the analogy of the broken phonograph record playing "I love you, I love you, I love you" over and over. Any parent who had that kind of thing going at home would have a nervous breakdown. But when a little tyke, just learning to talk, comes up and lisps, "Daddy, Mommy, I love you," that is worth the whole world.

Speaking of praise, I don't think that heaven is made up of people and angels spending all their time saying the same thing over and over and over again in unison. I've been trying to think this through after visiting a megachurch in Portland, Oregon, recently—how to structure a church program in such a way that everybody at every moment would always have the power of choice. I was somewhat flabbergasted at this megachurch in Portland, where everybody has to do the same thing at the same time. Is this what we want to pattern churches after?

I worked on college campuses for twenty years, and being around college students impressed me with one fact—students gripe a lot about all of the required church and chapel services. We were discussing this at our dinner table recently, and I remembered the pat answers I used to give these students who would come in with this complaint.

"We don't like all these required worships."

I would answer, "We don't have any required worships at this college."

They would exclaim, "Where have you been? What's wrong with you? Are you blind?"

"No, we don't have required worships," I would affirm. "You are not required to be here at this college at all."

They would go away with their heads hanging, and I would think that I had won. I'm not so sure.

Suppose that in heaven we found ourselves in a group of people or angels mimicking the same phrases of glory and praise over and over again. I wonder if we could say, "Wait a minute, I didn't choose to do this. I wanted to go hang gliding today without my hang glider." Would someone then say, "It's not required of you to do this. You weren't required to come here in the first place?"

I think that if heaven were a place where everyone did the same thing all the time, it would turn out to be hell instead. I think that heaven is going to be structured in such a way that everybody, at any moment and always, has the power of choice. That's what makes it heaven.

I wish that we could give some thought as to how we can do that with the services in our churches, so that people would feel comfortable at any moment, always having the power of choice. God has a sacred regard for that, because He knows the joy that comes from people who voluntarily and deliberately give praises to Him.

In 1 Corinthians 12:13–21 we find the church being compared to a human body. It is well known that the different members of the human body have a mutual concern for each other. When the tooth begins to ache, the eyes begin to look around for something to which the feet can take the person, so that the hand can open the bottle and put something in the mouth and help the pain that the tooth is experiencing. The eyes, the feet, and the hands do not say, "Well, the tooth can only blame itself for all these problems. It was the tooth that did the wrong thing and got the problem of aching." No, they all become concerned about each other. A simple scratch on a hand may not be serious at all, but if it is neglected by the rest of the body, it can become a serious problem.

Paul, by comparing the church to a body, helps us to understand a major principle of the church body. Like a physical body, it must hang together to be effective and helpful.

We might say that as long as we are together in spirit, we don't have to hang together in practice. But the only people who hang together in spirit are the ones who hang together in practice. It happens that way in a family. No family is together in spirit unless the members have the practice of being together on a regular basis. That's what relationships are based on. God sees that it's significant for us not to forsake the assembling of ourselves together. We get together regularly so that we can have unity of spirit and so that we can know about other members of the body of Christ and about their hurts and their needs.

Once in a while I hear people say, "I don't feel I have to go to church because I can get as much blessing at home." Others say, "I don't have to go to church. I can get as much blessing taking a walk in the woods." Or they say, "I can get as much good going down to the beach." The key phrase is "I can get . . ." "I can get . . ." "I can get . . ." That is the dead giveaway.

My son and his wife were still in college after they got married, and they had started following the practice of going to the beach or to the mountains on Sabbath instead of the church. They got more of a blessing that way, they thought, until the engine in their car had blown up for about the sixth time and the radiator was sending steam to the high heavens. As my son was standing by the side of the road stranded for the umpteenth time, he finally looked up toward heaven and said, "OK, God. I can take a hint." And they began going to church again. I don't know if God has angels that make radiators overflow or cause engines to blow up. My son and his wife discovered that there is a difference between always wanting to get and becoming involved in giving as well.

Notice another interesting thing about the church. It is an organized body. Can you imagine what would happen if my body wasn't organized? Perhaps, while speaking to an audience, I wanted to change microphones so that I could come closer to where the people are. My eyes would see a step down, but my feet would not cooperate. Have you ever tried to go straight ahead when there was a step down? We can understand a lot about the organization by looking at our own bodies with its parts working together in an organized way. As the body hangs together—the eyes see a door, the hand opens it, the feet walk through—things go well. If the organization breaks down, and the hand doesn't open the door and the face gets smashed, then things are not going so well. The body must hang together and be organized or there will be pandemonium.

I like to tell people who say things like "I can get more of a blessing in the woods than going to church" that they're going to die.

"What do you mean?" they ask in shock.

"You're going to die, that's it!" I confirm. Any member separated from the body is going to die. If you cut off the hand, it's going to die. If you cut off the foot and send it for a walk in the woods, it's going to die. In many species of lizard, if you cut off the tail, the lizard will grow another tail. But remember that a tail cannot grow another lizard. You need the body hanging together and the organization that the church can bring.

Many times in the past we have seen a group of people decide to start a new movement apart from the organic body of Christ. We have seen it die even though it sounded a lot like the gospel. People have tried and tried for centuries, and we have seen this happen in recent years too. It simply doesn't work. It's significant that the God of heaven has a keen interest in the body of Christ and continues to place value upon it.

I'd like to remind you of three things that a body does. First, a body eats. The whole body eats. You say no, it's the mouth that eats. But cut out the mouth and tell it to eat and it will not eat. Well, then, it's the stomach that eats. No, it's the mouth and the esophagus and the stomach together; it's the whole body that eats.

I don't know what part of the body you find yourself to be. Maybe you think you're the appendix or the tonsils, and you feel that you are dispensable. Maybe you're the head. Whatever you are, Paul says you are all important. Remember, it is the whole body that eats.

John 6:35 tells us that Jesus is the Bread of Life. We get together to eat the body of Christ, as Paul describes in 1 Corinthians 10:16, 17. "And is not the bread that we break a participation in the body of Christ?" This happens through God's Word.

A second thing a body does is breathe. Lamentations 3:55, 56 make it clear that the body breathes and that prayer is called breath. We read in the book *Steps to Christ* also that prayer is the breath of the soul (see page 99). The whole body breathes. When we get together in prayer as a body, we are doing some breathing that perhaps cannot be done in any other way, even though private prayer is significant and important.

The last of these three things the body does is exercise. Paul wrote, "Exercise thyself rather unto godliness" (1 Timothy 4:7, KJV). And here is where we are way behind. The *organized* exercising of the body is extremely important for it to be healthy and well. The organized church should spend some significant time considering its exercise program as a body. This would be frustrating if the church didn't even know who its members are. The midweek meeting is one place where the members can do their most creative things, working together to establish a goal and a direction for their mission, their outreach, and their service programs.

Jesus came back to Nazareth, where He was brought up, and as His custom was, He went into the synagogue on the Sabbath day. They gave Him the book, and He began to read. "The Spirit of the Lord is on me, because he has anointed me to preach good news to the poor." Why? Because the rich and the increased with goods won't hear you. "He hath sent me to heal the brokenhearted" (KJV). Why? Because only the brokenhearted realize their need of healing. And "to proclaim freedom for the prisoners." Why? Because only the prisoners in the world of sin realize their need of the One who came to set us free. "And recovery of sight for the blind." Why? Because it is only the blind who look for the light and long for the light—Jesus the Light of the world. And "to release the oppressed" or "to set at liberty them that are bruised" (Luke 4:18, KJV).

Do you find yourself battered and bruised by the enemy of our souls? One way Jesus promised to meet your needs is through His body, the church.

CHAPTER 3

THE WORK OF THE HOLY SPIRIT

I would like to share with you a little about the One who doesn't want us to talk about Him. As we encourage everyone to join in the work of the gospel in some way or another, I think it is important to notice that the Holy Spirit is very much involved.

Some people pay attention to the Holy Spirit in study circles, and once in a while we see a movement rising up that focuses just on Him. The truth is that He does not speak a whole lot about Himself. His sole purpose and mission is to focus attention on someone else. The Godhead works that way. If we look at it from a worldly standpoint, we might say it's some sort of a political agreement—you lift me up, and I'll lift you up. But it's far above that level when we're talking about the heavenly system. The Holy Spirit is obsessed with focusing our attention on Jesus, not on the Holy Spirit. We can end up on biblically troubled ground if we spend too much time on the Holy Spirit. We may even end up with the wrong spirit, if we don't listen to Scripture on the subject.

The work of the Holy Spirit is clearly divided into four areas. First of all, the Holy Spirit works to "convict the world of guilt in regard to sin" (see John 16:8). He *convicts* sinners, and He does this all the time. He does this even while we are sleeping.

The second work of the Holy Spirit is to *convert* the sinner (see John 3:5–9). He performs this work for sinners who are interested and open to Him, for those willing to put themselves in the atmosphere where it happens. Many new Christians live for a while with what is sometimes called the first love. If they do not go any further with their walk, they fade away.

It is too bad that only 20 to 25 percent continue on to allow the Holy Spirit to do His third work in them, that of *cleansing* the Christian. During this time, we open the door for Him by paying attention to personal fellowship, communication, quiet time, and devotional life day by day. If we do not participate in this fellowship with Christ day by day, then the third work of the Holy Spirit does not happen because He is not pushy, even though He is persistent. He comes in by invitation.

During the third work of the Holy Spirit, the cleansing work, the fruits of the Spirit begin to appear in our lives: "Love, joy, peace, patience, kindness, goodness, faithfulness, gentleness and self-control" (Galatians 5:22–23). These appear more and more as we grow in Christ.

Then we come to the fourth work of the Holy Spirit, which is *commission*—commission for service. Under the fourth work we receive the gifts of the Spirit, which include prophecy, healing, and the other gifts listed in 1 Corinthians 12 and 14. They are the mighty manifestations of the power of God through the Holy Spirit.

In summary, the four works of the Holy Spirit are (1) convict the world of sin; (2) convert the sinner; (3) cleanse the Christian; and (4) commission the Christian for service. The fourth work is the area on which I want to focus, which is the baptism with the Holy Spirit.

I was discussing this subject at a camp meeting, and afterward someone accosted me and said, "Why do you call it the baptism *with* the Holy Spirit? Why don't you call it baptism *of* the Holy Spirit?" Apparently they were nervous because it sounded like certain holiness groups involved in charismatic activities and maybe glossolalia. They didn't like the phrase "baptism with the Holy Spirit." I had to show from the Scriptures that that's what the Bible says—baptize *with* the Holy Spirit. There are many voices on this subject today, and if we're not careful to understand what the Bible says we can be misled. Many spirits are calling for our attention.

Luke is similar to the other Gospel writers, because they all record the same thing. Let's look at Luke 3:16: "John answered them all, 'I baptize you with water. But one more powerful than I will come, the thongs of whose sandals I am not worthy to untie. He will baptize you with the Holy Spirit and with fire.' " Here was a prediction made by the inspired John the Baptist. Was the prediction fulfilled? Did they remember it later?

Acts 1:4, 5, 8 tell us that they did. Jesus had already ascended to heaven, and His followers were missing Him, but they were excited about the promises they had heard. So they began reviewing what Jesus had told them.

> On one occasion, while he was eating with them, he gave them this command: "Do not leave Jerusalem, but wait for the gift my Father promised, which you have heard me speak about. For John baptized with water, but in a few days you will be baptized with the Holy Spirit. . . ."
> "But you will receive power when the Holy Spirit comes on you; and you will be my witnesses in Jerusalem, and in all Judea and Samaria, and to the ends of the earth."

In this scripture, the power is for witness. Power and witness, connected together, are very significant. If you trace through the words and phrases used in Scripture concerning the baptism with the Holy Spirit, you'll find several different ways of saying it. There is the promise of the Father. There is the promise that you will be endued with power from on high. And there is the promise that you will be filled with the Holy Spirit. Under the third work of the Holy Spirit, a filling takes place. Under the fourth work of the Holy Spirit, filling even to an overflowing takes place. Sometimes this is referred to as the gift of the Spirit, although this is not necessarily always referring to the baptism with the Holy Spirit.

Luke 24:49 gives Jesus' actual statement that they were reflecting on in the first chapter of Acts. Speaking just before He left them, Jesus said, " 'I am going to send you what my Father has promised; but stay in the city until you have been clothed with power from on high.' "

You know it when you have been baptized with the Holy Spirit. The disciples would have stayed in Jerusalem if they did not know it. Some say that the Holy Spirit is just sort of a general thing, not a noticeable phenomenon. But Jesus said, "Stay in the city *until* you have been clothed with power from on high." Others say that the Holy Spirit is present when we are baptized, and that's it. But in Acts we find people who have been baptized, and they are told to wait until they receive something further.

"Oh," some people say, "this is talking about the dispensation of the Holy Spirit, so we can't apply it today because that was talking about the inauguration of the Holy Spirit for special work. The disciples were to tarry until that day arrived, and then they would have something special." They also say it was different in the Old Testament than in the New, but you can't pass it off that way because the Holy Spirit was very much alive in the Old Testament. He was doing other things, like creation, but before the Day of Pentecost, He was very much alive and well. We're told also that John the Baptist was filled with the Spirit from his birth, and he was filled with the Spirit because his mother and father were filled with the Spirit. So it is not unheard of for people to experience the fullness of the Spirit over time.

For that reason we don't just pass off the role of the Holy Spirit after Pentecost as a difference in dispensation, as just the beginning of a new order. Jesus, in Old Testament times, exercised a quality that He sacrificed when He came to save us—His omnipresence. We really have no idea of the sacrifice Jesus made when He came, not only to die for us, but to remain a human being forever, one with us—called the Son of man in Revelation. The Holy Spirit does today what Jesus used to be able to do in person in Old Testament times.

This leads us to understand that the baptism with the Holy Spirit is a separate and distinct work from our conversion. We don't just say, "Well, the Holy Spirit was involved when I was baptized, and that's it." No, it's a separate and distinct work. Even so, we cannot take the position that the Holy Spirit is not involved in conversion, because He is. A significant text to help us understand the total involvement of the Holy Spirit in all of the Christian life is Romans 8:9: "You, however, are controlled not by the sinful nature but by the Spirit, if the Spirit of God lives in you. And if anyone does not have the Spirit of Christ, he does not belong to Christ." The Holy Spirit is involved all the way through the life of the Christian, from beginning to end.

At the same time let us remember that the Holy Spirit is not manifested in His fullness at conversion. When a person is born again, he or she has salvation and doesn't have to sit around worrying about that. But the person may not yet have all of the fullness of the Holy Spirit in terms of what God wants to do in his or her life.

I've heard people say that the apostle Peter wasn't converted because he went to the courtyard by the fire, denied Christ, and added cursing and swearing to it, which proved he had never been converted. This is the view of those who think that the minute you are converted you're supposed to never sin again, and if you sin again, that proves you've never been converted. This kind of mentality escapes me. I do not find it in Scripture at all. I find people who have been born again falling and failing and getting up and going on some more. Don't you? For sure, the apostles had been converted. How do I know? Because Peter had gone out with the others and had healed the sick, cast out devils, cleansed the lepers, and raised the dead. Unconverted people cannot do that in the presence of Christ. Peter was among those of whom Jesus said, "Rejoice that your names are written in heaven" (Luke 10:20).

Jesus is the One who said, "I tell you the truth, no one can see the kingdom of God unless he is born again" (John 3:3). So, when Jesus said to Peter, "And when you have turned back ["when thou art converted" in KJV], strengthen your brothers" (Luke 22:32), He was simply reminding him that conversion is a continuous experience, a renewal experience day by day. Here in the experience of Peter, who was a leading figure on the Day of Pentecost, we have someone who had been converted but had not yet experienced the baptism with the Holy Spirit in its fullness.

It's interesting to note Paul's experience recorded in Acts 19.

"While Apollos was at Corinth, Paul took the road through the interior and arrived at Ephesus. There he found some disciples and asked them, 'Did you receive the Holy Spirit when you believed?' They answered, 'No, we have not even heard that there is a Holy Spirit' " (Acts 19:1, 2).

I've always been amused at that answer. I identify with it because if someone were to come to me and say, "Have you received the Holy Ghost since you were converted?" it would be very easy to reply, "Oh! Hello? Did I miss something?" The Ephesian disciples said, "We have not even heard that there is a Holy Spirit." Paul was talking about something beyond the point of their becoming believers and being converted.

Paul asked them, " 'Then what baptism did you receive?' "

" 'John's baptism,' they replied.

"Paul said, 'John's baptism was a baptism of repentance. He told the people to believe in the one coming after him, that is, in Jesus.' On hearing this, they were baptized into the name of the Lord Jesus. When Paul placed his hands on them, the Holy Spirit came on them, and they spoke in tongues and prophesied" (Acts 19:3–5). This experience was separate and distinct from conversion.

Acts 8 gives us another interesting case in which people were baptized in the name of Jesus, this one about Philip, one of the early deacons. It's always exciting when a deacon wants to do more than "deac." We see that Stephen and others began to be preachers as well as deacons because they got their feet wet and, despite having stage fright, began to do something for God with the leading of the Holy Spirit. Here is Philip's story from Acts 8:12–17:

> When they believed Philip as he preached the good news of the kingdom of God and the name of Jesus Christ, they were baptized, both men and women. [Notice, this is about the baptism of Jesus Christ.] Simon himself believed and was baptized. And he followed Philip everywhere, astonished by the great signs and miracles he saw.
>
> When the apostles in Jerusalem heard that Samaria had accepted the word of God, they sent Peter and John to them. When they arrived, they prayed for them that they might receive the Holy Spirit.

Hadn't the Samaritans heard about Pentecost yet? Samaria isn't that far from Jerusalem. I traveled to Samaria from Jerusalem with Dr. Siegfried Horn several years ago. It's a very short distance. They must have heard about the Day of Pentecost. But here in this area of Samaria, Peter and John came to them and "prayed for them that they might receive the Holy Spirit, because the Holy Spirit had not yet come upon any of them; they had simply been baptized into the name of the Lord Jesus. Then Peter and John placed their hands on them, and they received the Holy Spirit."

This is another example from Scripture that the baptism with the Holy Spirit is a separate and distinct work beyond conversion.

We also have the experience of Cornelius in Acts 10. Cornelius sent for Peter, who was reluctant to go to his house because Cornelius was a Gentile. After seeing a vision, Peter ended up going, and he found a group of people who were already believers. When they listened to further truth, the Bible says,

> While Peter was still speaking these words, the Holy Spirit came on all who heard the message. The circumcised believers who had come with Peter were astonished that the gift of the Holy Spirit had been poured out even on the Gentiles. . . .
>
> Then Peter said, "Can anyone keep these people from being baptized with water? They have received the Holy Spirit just as we have." So he ordered that they be baptized in the name of Jesus Christ (Acts 10:44–48).

The experience of baptism with the Holy Spirit is separate and distinct and goes beyond conversion.

A third crucial point, according to Scripture, is that the baptism with the Holy Spirit is not for the purpose of making us holy or happy. These fruits have already happened in the life of those who are baptized with the Holy Spirit. Some people grossly misunderstand this. In fact, it is the big mark of demarcation between truth and falsehood concerning the baptism with the Holy Spirit. One of the best books I have ever read on the subject of the Holy Spirit is by R. A. Torrey, an associate of Dwight L. Moody. Torrey presented dynamic Bible truth concerning the Holy Spirit, and one time he got up on a public platform and said, "I'll give you ten thousand dollars for a text that shows me from Scripture that the baptism with the Holy Spirit is for any other reason than for making us useful."

What's wrong with the man from Phoenix, Arizona, that I heard about? He was discouraged with his life, the life of a defeated Christian. He was always beating up the kids and beating on his wife as well. He had a terrible temper. One day, he walked down the street thinking about the futility of it all and how he was ready to end it, and he passed a tent where people were getting the Holy Spirit. He wandered in, and before the meeting was over, he had the baptism with the Holy Spirit. Suddenly, his life was changed. His temper was gone. He didn't beat the children or the wife or break the furniture anymore. It was the wonderful work of the baptism with the Holy Spirit.

But, you say, what is wrong if his life was changed? Plenty! A changed life doesn't prove anything, because if I were the enemy I would be happy to change people's lives for a short time in exchange for something worse. That's why I ask people, If you had your choice of dying of cancer or being healed by the devil, what would you choose? If you had your choice of continuing to be a defeated Christian until God was able to do His work in your life, or being suddenly changed through the devil, what would you choose?

While I was a pastor in Colorado, a young fellow came to my office. He felt deep discouragement because he was going with a beautiful Christian young lady and she had discovered something he already knew about: his evil temper. He was going to lose her, and he was devastated. He said, "I heard that there are some meetings over at such-and-such church, and I was told that if I can get baptized with the Holy Spirit, my life will be changed."

I said, "Don't bother, because the baptism with the Holy Spirit is not to change your life. That's not its purpose. It is rather to help you change other people's lives."

When we lived in Modesto, we used to go down the street from our church to another church a block away. In this church people were getting holy and happy. It was our Saturday-night entertainment. We would stand outside and look through the windows and watch people getting holy and happy with the baptism of the Holy Spirit.

When I was in Japan, I shared with the director of student missions that I planned to visit the largest church in the world during my visit to Seoul, Korea. I was disappointed when he advised me not to go. I had been invited to Seoul for meetings and had planned to get there early and take in the largest church in the world. The director said, "It is a devastating experience to be in a church of thousands and thousands of people who suddenly all begin talking in tongues at the same time. This goes on for a while until someone gongs a bell, and they all quit talking when the bell gongs." We don't control the Holy Spirit by gonging bells. The Holy Spirit controls us.

This is the theology of the Holy Spirit: You will receive power for witness (for service) when the Holy Spirit comes on you (see Acts 1:8). So, if we are truly interested in the baptism with the Holy Spirit, we would have to take a long look at service. If we are involved in service, we can expect the Holy Spirit to be involved with us in a very special way.

In conclusion, let's take a look at twelve points concerning how to receive the baptism with the Holy Spirit:

1. Accept Jesus as your only hope of salvation—*all three* aspects of salvation: justification, sanctification, and glorification.
2. Repent of sin in your heart. And remember repentence is a gift from God to those who come to Him.

3. Know that you are converted. Can you know that you are converted? Yes, you can. You don't have to know the time or place, and often you won't. But you can know whether or not you have been converted. (see *Steps to Christ*, 58.)

4. Be baptized. The public confession of Christ is part of the process.

5. Consent for God to lead you to full surrender. Surrender is not giving up things; it is giving up on ourselves and depending totally on Jesus, which the growing Christian doesn't always do. You must be willing for God to lead you to absolute surrender, where you depend on Him all the time instead of part of the time.

6. Renounce all sin. Ouch! How can we do that? We're told in the book *Steps to Christ*, "We shall often have to bow down and weep at the feet of Jesus because of our shortcomings and mistakes" (64). How can you know if you're willing to renounce all sin? If you could press a button right now and never sin again, ask yourself, would you press the button? Or would you say, "Not so fast. It might change my lifestyle," or "It might spoil my fun." Do you trust God enough to press the button? It's a good way to ask yourself how ready you really are.

7. Become involved in service and witness.

8. Get thirsty for it. There is a promise for those who are thirsty. "Jesus stood and said in a loud voice, 'If anyone is thirsty, let him come to me and drink. Whoever believes in me, as the Scripture has said, streams of living water will flow from within him.' By this he meant the Spirit, whom those who believed in him were later to receive" (John 7:37-39).

9. Be in unity with your fellow Christians. Instead of being in the camp of those for whom good news means bad news

about other people, stay in unity and love with each other, because Jesus loves even the degraded and the unappealing.

10. Ask for it. The Scripture shows that it is important to ask for the blessings of God in humility in order to receive them.

11. Ask for the right motive. Why do I want the Holy Spirit? So I can raise the dead and send my picture to the papers so that they can see who did it? We can get the right motive only on our knees.

12. Believe that you have received it by trusting God's promise.

These are some of the points that the Bible is very clear on, I believe, concerning this tremendous experience of baptism with the Holy Spirit. Are you interested? Would you like to understand it more? Will you study it for yourself? I'd like to join you as we seek God's power for service.

CHAPTER 4

LIONS IN THE STREET

Have you ever seen lions in the street? While waiting for a flight at the airport in Nairobi, Kenya, heading toward South Africa, I looked and looked for a lion around the airport but couldn't find a single one. If you want to see lions in the street, look at the book of Proverbs.

Proverbs is a sort of theological cocktail. Don't try to do an in-context, exegetical study of Proverbs, because it jumps from here to there to the other place. But more than once, the author of Proverbs talks about the lions in the street. Let's take a look at two of them.

The first one is in Proverbs 26:13: "The sluggard says, 'There is a lion in the road, a fierce lion roaming the streets!' " The second is in chapter 22, verse 13: "The sluggard says, 'There is a lion outside!' or, 'I will be murdered in the streets!' " Aren't you thrilled with these texts? What kind of hope do they give you?

A homespun example of this would be when I tell my boy to take out the garbage and he says, "I can't do it. There is a lion out there." He uses it as an excuse. But what makes us slothful or a sluggard when it comes to Christian witness and service? Is it the lions out there in the street? As a matter of fact, there is a *big* one.

When I was in high school in Fresno, California, I worked in a gas station. My father became a faithful customer at the station, and some of the other guys I worked with picked up that he was a preacher, so they poked fun at him once in a while. One day when my dad dropped by, one of the guys who was servicing his car asked him,

"Well, Reverend, how is the big red devil today?"

My dad said without hesitation, "He is 'like a roaring lion looking for someone to devour.' So watch out that he doesn't get you!" Not too bad. There is a lion out there in the street.

There are many lions that keep us in by the fire, where we can keep our feet on the hassock, watch the fireplace, eat the apples and roast the marshmallows, and let someone else face the lions.

One time I asked an elder in my church,

"Give me the first three things that come to your mind as to why people find it difficult to get out and witness."

He said, "They don't know how." Then he added, "That's only an excuse. The real reason is that they are scared."

The first lion keeping us from going out is spiritual uncertainty. There is a high level of uncertainty in Christian circles. It is particularly high in my own subculture, because we have become famous for our emphasis on behavior as the bottom line for Christian faith. But this is not confined to us. Many, many people in the Christian church of all faiths are victims of this problem. If my primary emphasis in the Christian life is performance and behavior, if I think that my works have something to do with getting me to heaven, I'm going to be spiritually uncertain all the time, and I will not be excited about the things of the gospel, because I don't understand the gospel. This crippling problem can keep us off the street, preventing us from sharing, keeping us back in the fold with the other ninety-nine sheep.

What should we do about spiritual uncertainty? Is it possible for a spiritually uncertain reader who begins reading this chapter to find spiritual certainty as they arrive at the end of it? Or must they have ten years of good track record before they can go out with their heads up and face the lions? Do you believe it's possible to be certain of your own salvation by the end of this chapter? Or are you already certain of your own salvation?

We had some interesting discussions in our midweek meetings on this topic. We read a book by Neal Punt, the author I mentioned in chapter 1, who was challenging the evangelical world at large with the premise that he has biblical evidence that the whole world is saved except those who choose to be lost. This is the reverse of the premise the evangelical world has believed for a long time, that everyone is lost unless they choose to be saved.

You might say, "What difference does it make?" It makes a difference because of how it makes God look. God is responsible for us being born on planet Earth. Do you believe that God is doing everything He can to get people to heaven? Or do you believe that God is doing everything He can to keep people out of it? Can you take a text like the following one in 2 Peter and find spiritual certainty? "The Lord is . . . not willing that any should perish, but that all should come to repentance" (2 Peter 3:9, KJV). What about John 3:17, which follows the famous text? "For God did not send his Son into the world to condemn the world, but to save the world through him." There are texts that the apostle Paul is famous for, such as, "It is by grace you have been saved, through faith—and this not from yourselves, it is the gift of God—not by works, so that no one can boast" (Ephesians 2:8, 9); and, "Now when a man works, his wages are not credited to him as a gift, but as an obligation. However, to the man who does not work but trusts God who justifies the wicked, his faith is credited as righteousness" (Romans 4:4, 5). Do you believe that our works have nothing whatever to do with causing us to be saved? If you believe that, you can have spiritual certainty. If it is *His* works that cause me to be saved and not my works, I can get up and go out in the streets.

Do you believe that your bad deeds and your disobedience have nothing whatsoever to do with causing you to be lost? That's a hard one. I believe that. It took me a while to get that into my system, because I just wasn't programmed that way. Somewhere along the line, I thought that my bad works had a lot to do with causing me to be lost. No, there is only one reason why anyone is saved or lost—how they relate to the Lord Jesus Christ, whether they accept Him as their only hope or whether they walk away from a relationship with Him day by day.

An ordinary person with no hope could hear these words today and find hope, because Jesus is the hope of our eternal destiny. It is nothing that we can do. Our good works are simply the results of accepting that hope. Our bad works are simply the results of not accepting that hope. If we truly accept it into our hearts and lives we can have spiritual certainty today that will get us away from that big lion out in the streets that keeps us by the fire.

2nd A second lion that makes people stay away from the flashing lights and the bustling throng is fear of getting driven into a theological corner. "I don't know all the key texts," they say, or "I don't know all the ways to prove what I believe." "Someone might ask me a question that I can't answer." Great models of those who know the Bible backward and forward make it even scarier. I've heard people tell about those who have the Bible practically memorized and those who have read it a hundred times and those who could simply reproduce it from their photographic memories. That's enough to make you want to stay home by the fireplace.

I'll never forget the surprise I had when I first had the privilege of walking into the presence of H. M. S. Richards, Sr., a mild, humble quiet man. Those who were the closest to him knew he was like that. Yet he was a famous radio preacher. Amazingly, though, when I was alone with him, *I* was the great radio preacher, *I* was the theologian, *I* was the Bible expert, and he was the simple learner at my feet. I've never been able to explain that. It happened every time I had a chance to talk to him. He always made me feel as though he was learning from me. I felt as though I was ten feet tall, and whenever I left his presence, I had to go back to what I was before. It was very disappointing.

During our conversations, I heard him say more than once, "I don't know. I don't know." Do you know what it does to you when someone asks you a question and they think you're supposed to be the authority and you say, "I don't know"? Does it do damage? Or do they respect you for it? There is nothing wrong with saying, "I don't know, but I'll try to find out." In fact, there is everything right about that. So let's get away from thinking that only the experts can do it.

There is something else wrong with being afraid to witness because we may be driven into a theological corner. It is wrong because this fear is based on the false premise that the primary thing we witness to is twenty-seven points of church belief. But that's not our primary witness. A witness is someone who personally witnessed something. So don't ask me to try and be a witness on the state of the dead because I haven't been there yet. Don't ask me to be a witness on hell fire, hopefully. But you can ask me to be a witness on what Jesus means to me.

Let's not forget the demoniacs, who are the classic examples of being a witness. They came to Jesus naked, and they must have left with some clothes that came either from the Dorcas Society or off people's backs, one of the two. The evidence is that the clothes came from the disciples. These poor men, who had been naked among the tombs, cutting themselves and screaming and screeching, suddenly were in their right minds again. Jesus said to them, "Go tell your friends." Tell them what? Tell them about the state of the dead and the twenty-three-hundred years and the sanctuary and the judgment? No. Jesus said, "Go tell your friends how much the Lord has done for you, and how He has had mercy on you" (see Mark 5:19). (See also Luke 8:38, 39.) That is the personal basis for Christian witness and the number-one way to get involved in service. That is what we do to help people. We share what Jesus means to us, what He has done for us.

The little book *Steps to Christ*, which is a classic on the subject, says that when we have tasted and seen that the Lord is good, we will have something to tell about what a wonderful friend we have found in Jesus (see page 78).

3   The third lion out there in the streets may be where the real problem lies. That is the problem of success. Who can measure success when it comes to witnessing? This is so nebulous, yet we try to make it concrete. We almost get it down to the numbers game. But the Christian church, ours and everybody else's, is drunk today on the whole idea of church growth, which is always measured by statistical and numerical factors. Is that the way God looks at it? In a little paper called the *Southern Watchman*, I read something that said, "the Lord is good. . . . He knows just what each of us is doing. He knows just how much credit to give each one. Will you not lay down your credit list and . . . leave God to do His own work?" (May 14, 1903). Only God knows what success is.

Sometimes we have some big surprises. Years ago in Colorado, a preacher pitched a tent in a little town, where he held some meetings. He preached his heart out, worked hard, visited with people in their homes, and gave many Bible studies. At the end of the meetings, there was only one convert. He baptized the one convert and went on his way, licking his wounds. All his efforts seemed to be a big failure. Nobody knew until years later that this preacher, H. M. S. Richards, Sr., had baptized the father of George Vandeman, who founded the It Is Written television ministry and served as primary evangelist and director for more than thirty years.

Nobody knows until years later, maybe even centuries later on the streets of a better country, what really happened in terms of success. That is God's department, not ours. Can we accept that? I don't really know what is going on behind the scenes, in people's hearts, and that's why we are told in that same little book, talking about the humblest and poorest disciples of Jesus, "They are not required to weary themselves with anxiety about success" (*Steps to Christ*, 83). Yet that is probably one of the reasons we are afraid. We find this formidable lion out in the street. We are afraid of failing, afraid of a lack of success.

I think that it would be well for us to spend some time in prayer asking God to help us to leave the results in God's department. God won't say in the end, "Well done, thou good and successful servant." He will say, "Well done, good and *faithful* servant!" (Matthew 25:21). There seems to be quite a difference in man's estimation.

A fourth lion in the street, which is another "biggie," has been brought to my attention recently. I had looked away and around the corner for a long time, but it is becoming front and center now. The more I talk with people and the more case histories come into focus, the more I believe it is true. A lion that would keep us from going out is the usual reason that we give for going out. In other words, the very reason we have given in the Christian church for witnessing is what keeps us from witnessing.

Let's say that a minister of music comes to me and says, "I want you to be responsible for the cantata next year." You know what I would say? "I'm gone. I just left town." Suppose God came to me and said, "I want you to go out and witness because souls are going to be saved or lost if you do, or don't." You know what I would say? "I'm out of here. Leave me out. That's beyond me." If I were to try and put together a cantata for next year, not only would the success of the program come into focus and become a real heavy burden to bear, but another factor would come up, that I do not want to bobble and perhaps ruin people's lives with my mistakes.

If I believe that the primary purpose for my going out in service and witness is to save souls, that thought will keep me from going out! Because I don't want to bobble. I don't want to ruin it for others, and I am afraid I will ruin it. So instead I will let the professionals handle everything.

If I believe that someone's eternal destiny is totally in God's hands regardless of what I do, then I can go out and not be afraid of bobbling. I can make mistakes without having to worry about that anymore. I can actually relax and enjoy going out, knowing that that lion in the street has been taken care of.

This is an ironic premise, but I believe there is truth to it. I do not believe that anyone's eternal destiny is based upon what I do or don't do. Therefore, I am free to witness even if my witness seems feeble.

There is a chapter in *The Desire of Ages* that contains this comment: "Angels of heaven are passing throughout the length and breadth of the earth, seeking to comfort the sorrowing, to protect the imperiled, to win the hearts of men to Christ. Not one is neglected or passed by" (639). What an ego trip we might be on to think that we are the only ones involved in the work of the gospel. We are like that little three-year-old of mine who puts his hands on the lawnmower and thinks he did the mowing when his daddy did the whole job. Let's not be so naive as to think that we are going to finish God's work. The angels are involved. "Not one is neglected or passed by. God is no respecter of persons, and He has an equal care for all the souls He has created" (ibid). Here is another reason we can go out and witness without worring about our mistakes. If I ruin things in my witness, God will send you along to fix it up for me, and if you ruin it, He will send someone else along. If they don't go, the angels will go, and if they don't, the stones will cry out.

In the same chapter of *The Desire of Ages,* there is this quote: "Those whom Christ commends in the judgment may have known little of theology, but they have cherished His principles. . . . Among the heathen are those who worship God ignorantly, those to whom the light is never brought by human instrumentality, yet they will not perish. Though ignorant of the written law of God, they have heard His voice speaking to them in nature, and have done the things that the law required. Their works are evidence that the Holy Spirit has touched their hearts, and they are recognized as the children of God" (638). Does God have an equal regard for all the souls He has created? I believe He does, otherwise He wouldn't be a God of love.

I believe the following verses include women and children as well as men: "For the grace of God that brings salvation has appeared to all men" (Titus 2:11). "The Spirit of God is freely bestowed to enable every man to lay hold upon the means of salvation." *The Great Controversy* goes on to say, "Thus Christ, 'the true Light,' 'lighteth every man that cometh into the world.' John 1:9. Men fail of salvation only through their own willful refusal of the gift of life" (262). Anyone who is saved or lost will have made that choice himself, based upon whatever light he understood and not based on your success or your bobbles in witnessing.

I have heard some say that people are going to point their fingers at us in the judgment and say, "I'm lost because of you." Yes, they're going to do that. And do you know what God is going to say? "Not so!" or something like that. Just because people cast the blame upon me for being responsible for them being lost, doesn't mean that's why they are lost.

So we in the Christian church need to have victory over the idea that the primary purpose of witnessing is to save the lost, or we will never go out and do it. That is one of the big lions in the streets. Who is going to be lost if we don't go out and do it? We are. God's purpose for the Christian witness is to save us.

I have always been grateful to those students in algebra class who would come to me thinking that I understood those problems and would ask me to show how to solve them. Do you know what having to help them did for me? It made me work on finding out how to solve these problems for myself and helped me succeed in algebra. If you have ever tried to help someone else understand something and ended up understanding it better, you know what I mean. If you don't understand the Sabbath School lesson for this week, and you don't understand it for next week, sign on to teach it next week. You will understand it by next week. That is why God gave us a part to act in Christian service and witness. And we can go with assurance, knowing that our efforts will be blessed. Just remember that they will not make any eternal difference for others. God has that in His hands.

It is easy in this computer age to find all the texts on a certain topic or word, so I found one other text that has lions in it, an interesting verse in the book of Amos. "Woe to you who long for the day of the LORD! Why do you long for the day of the LORD? That day will be darkness, not light. It will be as though a man fled from a lion only to meet a bear, as though he entered his house and rested his hand on the wall only to have a snake bite him" (Amos 5:18, 19). The day of the Lord will be darkness and not light, unless you have accepted His grace. That's the context of Amos. You have the privilege of accepting the gift of repentance, and if you don't, the day of the Lord is going to be nothing more than a lion in the street. You run from the lion only to meet a bear, and you run into the house and the serpent bites you. Whether I am comfortable by the fire or comfortable in the fold with the ninety and nine is beside the point, because something is going to get me if I don't get involved with Jesus and the work of the gospel.

I traveled for several days in Kruger National Park in South Africa, trying to see the sights and sounds of the wildlife in Africa. For three days I looked for a lion and never saw one. I finally took a picture of a man who had seen one. That was the closest I got to it. But I've seen plenty of lions around the Christian church. Have you? They are there. I'm thankful that there is Someone bigger than they are.

Have you heard about the lion stalking through the jungle? He put his head down and roared,

"Who's king of the jungle?"

All of the animals shouted, "You are! You are!"

He went up to a giraffe and asked, "Who is king of the jungle?" The giraffe didn't respond. So the lion jammed into him and gave him a whiplash. (That would be a terrible thing, wouldn't it, for a giraffe to get a whiplash?)

Then the lion went on through the jungle until he came to where the elephants gather, and out there in the field, he put his head to the ground, roared, and said,

"Who's the king of the jungle?"

The elephants just kept on eating, so the lion tried again. He went up to an elephant and swatted him in the trunk.

"Who's the king of the jungle?" he shouted. At that point the elephant took his trunk and wound it around the lion. Then he slung the lion through the air and tossed him up twenty feet high. The lion came down with a splat on the ground. The elephant got on top of him and danced a Russian folk dance. After that was done, the lion stood up painfully and walked away, moaning, "You don't have to act like that just because you don't know the answer."

Even though we have an enemy, a roaring lion seeking whom he may devour, there is Someone bigger than he is. God has made provision to send him on his way. He has already conquered. We don't have to be afraid of lions in the streets anymore, and we can sign on for service and witness knowing that we serve Someone bigger.

Tuesday 1-17-06

CHAPTER 5

FISHING ON THE RIGHT SIDE

When I was a little boy I learned a song that helped me learn the names of all twelve disciples. It goes like this:

> "There were twelve disciples
> Jesus called to help Him:
> Simon Peter, Andrew,
> James, his brother John;
> Philip, Thomas, Matthew,
> James, the son of Alphaeus;
> Thaddeus, Simon, Judas, and Bartholomew."

The chorus is simple:

> "He has called us too,
> He has called us too.
> We are His disciples;
> I am one, and you."

Repeat the chorus then end with:

"We His work must do."

Do you like that? The next time you're on a hundred-thousand-dollar quiz program and they ask you to name the twelve disciples, just sing it out and bring what you get back to your church, please.

I don't know if you like fishing stories. I've never been much into fishing myself. I thought I'd try it one time, so I took a safety pin and put some watermelon on it. I hung it on a string and, believe or not, I caught a fish. I felt so bad about it that, when I finally got that thing out of his throat, I let him go, and I felt better.

Luke tells a fishing story that will surpass all of them.

One day as Jesus stood by the Lake of Gennesaret, with the people crowding around him and listening to the word of God, he saw at the water's edge two boats, left there by the fishermen, who were washing their nets. He got into one of the boats, the one belonging to Simon, and asked him to put out a little from shore. Then he sat down and taught the people from the boat.

When he had finished speaking, he said to Simon, "Put out into deep water, and let down the nets for a catch."

Simon answered, "Master, we've worked hard all night and haven't caught anything. But because you say so, I will let down the nets."

When they had done so, they caught such a large number of fish that their nets began to break. So they signaled their partners in the other boat to come and help them, and they came and filled both boats so full that they began to sink.

When Simon saw this, he fell at Jesus' knees and said, "Go away from me, Lord; I am a sinful man!" For he and all his companions were astonished at the catch of fish they had taken, and so were James and John, the sons of Zebedee, Simon's partners.

Then Jesus said to Simon, "Don't be afraid; from now on you will catch men." So they pulled their boats up on shore, left everything and followed him (Luke 5:1–11).

John 21: 1-7

This is a fisherman's story that is not fishy. It is full of truth.

"Years ago my father saw a notice in the front window of a sporting goods store, an ode to the typical fisherman written in old English:

'Behold the fisherman, he ariseth a great while before day and disturbeth the whole household. Mighty are his preparations. He goeth forth with great expectations, and when the day is far spent, he returneth filled with strong drink, and the truth is not in it.' "

I've heard some big fishermen stories in my life, and I've seen them get bigger and bigger. I suppose you have too. But when you read this story in Luke, you realize this is truth that impressed even these men who were veterans of the ships, the nets, and the sea. *1½ years* This happened about a year and a half into Jesus' ministry.

John 21 records a similar story, which took place after three and a half years of Jesus' ministry on earth, just before He went back to heaven. From the story we get another phrase that is really interesting for the Christian witness. Jesus had concluded His ministry, the Crucifixion had passed, He was meeting the people He'd promised to meet in Galilee, and He showed Himself to His disciples. This is what John writes:

3½ pro Years Afterward Jesus appeared again to his disciples, by the Sea of Tiberias. It happened this way: Simon Peter, Thomas (called Didymus), Nathanael from Cana in Galilee, the sons of Zebedee, and two other disciples were together. "I'm going out to fish," Simon Peter told them, and they said, "We'll go with you." So they went out and got into the boat, but that night they caught nothing.

Early in the morning, Jesus stood on the shore, but the disciples did not realize that it was Jesus.

He called out to them, "Friends, haven't you any fish?"

"No," they answered.

He said, "Throw your net on the right side of the boat and you will find some." When they did, they were unable to haul the net in because of the large number of fish.

Then the disciple whom Jesus loved said to Peter, "It is the Lord!" (John 21:1–7). *Luke 5:1–11*

"It is the Lord." What a revelation! What a thrill for them, who had been lonely and wondering. What a joy it was, especially for Peter with his sorrow, his disappointment, and his broken heart because he felt that he had brought the greatest grief to Jesus in His denial. What a joy it was for him to hear John say, "It is the Lord." Apparently at that point, Peter wasn't wearing much clothing. So he put something on, jumped into the lake, and swam to Jesus, because he couldn't wait to get to the shore.

Let's take a look at a few of the phrases that show up in these two stories. First of all Jesus told the disciples, before they had any success, to launch out into the deep. Here we have something of spiritual significance. Our own experience may be just shallow enough that we find it hard to do the right kind of fishing. In that case, we need to consider something like Ephesians 3, where Paul told us that we have the privilege of having an experience characterized by height, length, breadth, and depth. He says, "So that Christ may dwell in your hearts through faith. And I pray that you, being rooted and established in love, may have power, together with all the saints, to grasp how wide and long and high and deep is the love of Christ, and to know this love that surpasses knowledge, that you may be filled to the measure of all the fullness of God" (Ephesians 3:17–19).

Perhaps one of the greatest preparations we could consider for being able to go fishing with Christ is to launch out into a deeper experience with Him, instead of staying with the shallow text for the day with your hand on the doorknob, or the "Christmas and Easter" syndrome. Deeper yet, as we sometimes sing, so that we have fresh in our own hearts the excitement of the gospel and can join the song of those angels over the plain who couldn't keep still but sang "glad tidings with great joy." Launch out into the deep.

Then Jesus said, "Let down *your* nets" (Luke 5:4, KJV, emphasis added). For a long time we've had the evangelist's net, the colporteur's net, the professional's net, and the communal church net. We have tried to catch people, and we have neglected to notice this key word *your*. It seems to me that for a long time church members have been geared to standing in the wings or sitting in the bleachers and watching while those on center stage go fishing. The appeal to us here is "He has called us too." He has called you too. We are all His disciples, and "we His work must do."

Once I read about a great evangelistic push in a town in Ohio. Some evangelical churches got together and figured out that there were 135,000 people in their town. They figured that there were probably 50,000 who were old enough to be saved but were without Christ. They held a six-week evangelistic campaign led by one of the most capable and widely sought-after evangelists in the land. The campaign was cooperated in most heartily by more than fifty churches, resulting in reaching about 1,200 souls. This was cause for great rejoicing.

But what did the churches do for the other 49,000 souls who were still outside of Christ? Nothing. They had spared neither labor nor expense to give the lost of their city the chance of their lifetime to come to the gospel and be saved, so what more could they do? They had done their utmost to get the sheaves to come out of the fields to be harvested, to get the fish to come to shore to be caught, to get the dead to come to life. And if 49,000 of them insisted on staying away, the church was helpless to do more. Isn't that right?

When we think of fishing, most of us can picture a man sitting by the river on a lazy summer day, leaning against a tree with his hat pulled over his face, sound asleep. The string is tied around his big toe, and he is waiting for a fish to come. Maybe that's a more accurate picture of the common practice of the Christian church. Are we supposed to wait for the fish to come and get caught when the evangelist comes to town? That's the penetrating question.

Here is where we get into the significance of casting *our* nets—my net and your net. The evangelist couldn't go out and rub shoulders with all of the people that those townspeople rub shoulders with. The modern approach, which is the sensible approach, is for Christian service and Christian witness to be a way of life, not a program. It is a lifestyle, not something that we strategize once a year or once every three years to do from the center stage. "Launch out into the deep, and let down *your* nets" (Luke 5:4, KJV, emphasis added), Jesus said.

What about your net? How is it working? Are you involved? Are you interested in getting involved? I think most of us are interested. I have taken surveys of hundreds of people, young and old. Somewhere along the line, the top five questions include this one: "How can I learn to be an effective witness in the Christian church?" One of the first things we can do is realize that each of us has a net.

Jesus said to the disciples, " 'Throw your net on the *right* side of the boat and you will find some' " (John 21:6, emphasis added). I need to point out that there is a difference, for practical purposes, between Christian service and Christian witness. Christian service means getting involved with people in humanitarian ways, helping people in need. Christian witness is what we do with our tongues and with our lives, in relationship to Jesus, once we have reached the people with service. The purpose of service is to lead us into witness. Christian service is no substitute for witness, but it can be an easy escape from witness. This becomes a little clearer when we see the two of them going together. This is casting the net on the right side of the ship.

"Simon answered, 'Master, we've worked hard all night and haven't caught anything' " (Luke 5:5). Well, what good was that? What point is there in toiling all night and catching nothing? You might as well sit by the tree with your hat over your face and the string tied around your big toe. At least you get a little rest and relaxation instead of toiling all night and taking nothing. Or is there a benefit to the toil? Is it worthwhile to work hard all night and catch nothing? What about the person who flunks the exam and then studies like he's never studied before and passes with honors next time? When my major professor, Dr. Heppenstall, was in college, he got up to give a speech in speech class one day, and halfway through his speech the professor shouted from the back of the room, "Heppenstall, sit down. That is the worst speech I have ever heard." Heppenstall was so angry that he went to work and ended up giving the class speech at the end of the semester.

What about the person who loses the race and trains harder than ever before and wins the next one? What about the person who goes for the physical examination and flunks the treadmill test, and as a result gets involved in an exercise program and becomes interested in physical fitness? It is not all bad to toil all night and take nothing because it might motivate you to something better.

These disciples toiled all night and took nothing, and they were discouraged. Maybe they had experienced it before and just said, "You win some, you lose some." But one thing is certain: They were not feeling particularly self-sufficient or flushed with fish. Perhaps they were open to depending upon someone else. Jesus said, "Put out into deep water, and let down the nets for a catch."

After they had given their objection—"We have toiled all night and have taken nothing"—someone came in with the right response: "But because you say so, I will let down the nets." Remember that we, as a Christian church, have toiled all night and have taken nothing, when we consider the needs of the world. I have seen the statistics showing us that the world population is still growing faster than we are taking the gospel to them. That includes all Christian churches toiling together, not just the one that is familiar with the three angels.

I have heard the counterargument that this is not true. Some want to say that we've had tremendous success and that we've just about finished the work. Others say, wait a minute, let's be real. We have toiled all night and taken nothing.

What is the purpose of service and witness anyway? Why did God give us this work to do? That is a significant question. Have you thought in your mind as to why God gave us the privilege of service and witness? For whose sake is it?

God gave that privilege for our sake. It isn't for someone else to go to center stage and do the work while we applaud his success.

A preacher came to a church in Buenos Aires, Argentina, that had 184 members. He said, "We got to work right away, and after two years of vigorous organizing and outreach we were up to around six hundred. We had tripled in size. Our follow-up system was one of the best. The denomination was so impressed that I was invited," said the pastor, "to be a main speaker at two different conventions, to share my follow-up system and distribute samples of all our forms. Yet underneath it all I sensed that something wasn't right. Things seemed to stay high as long as I worked sixteen hours a day. But when I relaxed, everything came down. That disturbed me. Finally, I decided to stop."

He added, "I told my board I must go away for two weeks to pray. I headed for the countryside and gave myself to meditation and prayer. The Holy Spirit began to break me down. The first thing He said was, 'You are promoting the gospel the same way Coca Cola sells Coke, the same way Reader's Digest sells books and magazines. You are using all the human tricks you learned at school. But where is My hand in all of this?' I didn't know what to say. Then the Lord told me a second thing. 'You are not growing,' He said. 'You think you are because you've gone from two hundred to six hundred. You are not growing. You are just getting fat.' "

The person who finds himself getting fat because of lack of exercise faces a tremendous challenge in accepting what Jesus said when He told the disciples, "Follow Me and I will make you fishers of men." Accept the fact that we have tended to be spectators instead of participants and that we have missed out on growth for that reason.

This preacher in Buenos Aires continued telling about how he began to try and listen to what it means to let down the net at God's word, at Jesus' word. Instead of thinking of human planning and human gimmicks, he began to listen carefully for God's voice and to follow His reasons and His plans, to "cast the net on the right side of the boat."

The amazing thing about these stories is that we find the right side was actually the wrong side. The book *The Desire of Ages,* on the life of Christ, suggests that Jesus was on the shore and the disciples were in the boats when He said, "Cast the net on the right side," which would have been the side toward Jesus. That's not a bad idea, to cast the net on the side where Jesus is.

After catching nothing all night, the disciples knew, when Jesus told them to cast the net on the right side, that this was not the right time of day to fish. They also knew that the right side, the side Jesus was indicating, was actually the wrong side for fishing. This is often the case; the right side is the wrong side, according to human logic and reason. Think of all the times in Scripture when God invited people to do foolish things in order to fulfill His purpose—strange things that just didn't make sense.

But these disciples were open to their Lord and Master, at least by this time. And Peter said, "Because You say so, I will let down the nets."

I suggest that casting the net on the right side is following God's plans; it is going to our knees and listening to what His plans are, instead of our own strategies. Casting the net on the right side, as far as the church is concerned, means realizing that each one of us has a net, and that witness and service has as its source people who have been there.

What do I mean by that? Imagine that your friend next door saw an accident downtown, and he is called in to court to give witness to the accident. But he's sick that day, so he writes out twenty-seven points about the accident and gives them to you to go and show up in court for him. (I know this could not really be done.) You go down to the court, the bailiff swears you in, an attorney asks you about the accident, and you give the twenty-seven points. But you don't realize until it begins to happen that you're going to be asked some questions about the points. And when they begin asking questions, all you can do is go, "Ooh, oooh." Why? Because you weren't there.

Then the attorney asks, "Are you a witness?"

"Well, no," you reply. "The witness is sick today, and he sent me instead with these twenty-seven points." And they dismiss you from court along with the twenty-seven points.

Have you ever heard of the twenty-seven points? What have you experienced of these twenty-seven points? Experiencing these twenty-seven points, not just reciting them, is casting the net on the right side of the boat. Witnessing is personal. You can't talk about it unless you have been there. You can't share with someone else what you have not experienced yourself. What a challenge to the Christian church and to every member. Casting the net on the right side of the boat, as far as the church of Christ is concerned, is realizing that He has called us to witness about what we have seen and experienced. Everyone is involved.

Jesus enlarged the Christian commission, the gospel commission, from a small group, to a larger one, to an even larger one. First you have one or two who are following Him. Then you have three or four, after that the twelve, the seventy, then a hundred and twenty. Finally, after the Crucifixion, He meets with five hundred people in Galilee. They came from different places and for different reasons. Some doubted, and some believed. But they heard that He was going to meet them there.

If you read about the gospel commission in its fullness, you will notice that it was given to every person who hears. This is what has gotten me away from fear and procrastination. Anyone who feels the call to let down their net into the deep has the support and the credentials, or whatever is considered important by the church, because the gospel commission is given to everybody. I understand that before it's all over, even the little children are going to be involved in amazing ways.

The disciples let down the net into the deep on the right side of the ship, and then the success factor came in. The success factor—ouch! Most of us can't stand a success. In fact, I read one of the warnings written to some of our church leaders long ago that success destroys more often than it doesn't, and that in nine cases out of ten, anyone who has a degree of success, even in God's work, becomes independent and self-sufficient. God can no longer use them. That's a tragic reality, but it's the truth.

If we were to turn the town upside-down, we would want to be sure that the world knew about it. Wouldn't we? Send the statistics in to the world headquarters. Get a picture so we can advertise who was responsible. If I were able to raise someone from the dead, of course I would want people to know about the one who was raised from the dead and also about the one who did the raising. Most of us cannot be trusted with the power of God; it would destroy us.

In both passages we suddenly see ships that are filled with fish. That sounds like success, but the boats begin to sink. What is the boat? It is the church. What is the net? The net is the gospel. The net brings the fish into the church. Here we can see something important: We begin to sink the minute we begin looking at *our* achievements or our goals that we have reached, and we leave God off in the distance somewhere, waiting in the shadows.

One man in these stories related to the situation in the right way. When he heard from his compatriot, "It is the Lord," he plunged into the water and swam to Jesus. On one occasion, it says, "He fell at Jesus' knees and said, 'Go away from me, Lord; I am a sinful man!' " The picture looks something like this: He is pleading for Jesus to depart, but at the same time he's holding on for dear life to Jesus' feet and ankles.

Isaiah sees a picture of God high and lifted up, and his reaction is, "Woe is me, for I am a sinful man and I dwell with the people who are sinful. We're unclean. How can we stand to be in Your presence?" But he holds on. This happens again and again in the life of godly people. When they realize it is the Lord, they feel uneasy, but they hang on. Then they realize that God wants them to hang on. Aren't you glad He wants you to?

We can say with Peter, "Depart from me. In Your presence, in Your purity, in Your might, in Your power, in the demonstration of what You're able to do, I feel like nothing." And that's not a bad place to be. The highest place that we can achieve is bowing low at the foot of the cross. That's the highest place you'll ever get. And that's where Peter found himself that day. He said, "Depart from me, Lord, for I am a sinful man." But Jesus did not depart, even though He went away. He sent His Holy Spirit to be with us to this very moment.

The conclusion of the story says that they brought their ships to land. They parked them there and forsook all. Earlier in the story, in the first experience, the disciples had been on-again, off-again followers of Jesus. Perhaps they went back once in a while to fish for fun or R&R. Perhaps they went back to get some clothes and food for the family. But now, it says, "they pulled their boats up on shore, left everything, and followed him" (Luke 5:10, 11). Whenever you read the phrase, "Follow Me," or read about people following Jesus, you can usually see in it the atmosphere of witness, of service, of reaching out to others.

Jesus said, "Don't be afraid; from now on you will catch men" (Luke 5:10) and women and children. Don't be afraid. Are you ever afraid? I'm afraid when I have to get up and preach. I'm basically painfully shy. I'm bashful. If anyone could preach, you could, but I couldn't. I'm at the bottom of the heap as far as being able to preach.

I was working with a chaplain who is a born extrovert, if I ever saw one. I told him that he makes me sick. There is a genuine extrovert, I said, and there is a fake extrovert. The genuine extrovert gets energy from the crowd. He would be exhausted if he was alone. The fake extrovert gets strained by the crowd, and he gets energy when he is alone. Guess which I am? I'm so jealous. But we're all different. Some of the people we think are the most out-going are shyer than we realize. So if you're afraid, welcome to the club.

Jesus said, in the setting of the fishing and the nets and the gospel commission, "Fear not. Take My yoke upon you." Taking a yoke sounds like work. But, He says, in the end, "My yoke is easy and My burden is light."

I tried to sell books out in the plains of Nebraska. I had to do that one summer, putting in the four hundred hours required of ministerial students. Monday mornings were the worst. They were just awful! I would wash my car, polish my shoes, sharpen my pencils, and then I would wash my car, polish my shoes, and go through the whole routine all over again. Monday mornings, try-ing to get started out there with the nets—have you experienced that? But once you get into it, once you get involved, you find out the yoke that you thought was all hard work becomes easy, the burden becomes light, and the excitement comes on. Have you ever noticed this? It is true. That's the way it works.

I invite you to think seriously about the privilege we have of getting involved with the disciples out there on the sea. We can pray that God will help us cast the net on the right side of the boat.

CHAPTER 6

HOLY SWEAT

I've done a lot of research and careful investigation to find out who is the most miserable person on earth. Would you like to know who it is? The most miserable person on earth is the one whose life is most turned in on itself.

I'm also glad to know who the happiest person is. Do you know the answer already? Based on a timeless and universal principle, you don't even have to look in the Good Book to find out. Ann Landers talked about it, and so did her sister and countless others. The happiest person on earth is the one whose life is the most directed towards serving others. That's what makes angels happy. That's what makes heaven heaven.

God knew what He was doing when He gave us a chance to be dues-paying members of society, of the human race. While I was a pastor in Grand Terrace, California, one of my associate pastors, Rich Dubose, said he wanted to have a creative ministry fair, complete with balloons and everything.

He said, "I would like for you to preach on that subject."

"What subject is that?" I asked.

He answered, "Holy sweat."

"I beg your pardon!" I questioned. "What is holy sweat?"

He handed me a book and said, "Here, you can read about it in this book by Tim Hansel. The purpose of the book is to find out our high calling in Christ and the sweat it takes to get there."

When I first heard about holy sweat, I thought it had to do with the old sacrificial system, when the priests spent all day with the burned offerings and sacrifices, which probably produced a lot of holy sweat. I also thought of it as a secular word used in our everyday conversations, something like perspiration.

Then I punched the word *sweat* into my computer using a Bible program and discovered that only three texts in the Bible mention this word. The word "holy" shows up 584 times in the New International Version. (I'm sure you are thrilled with this information.) The first time the Bible mentions the word *sweat* is in Genesis 3:19, where Adam was leaving the Garden and his sentence was pronounced: "By the sweat of your brow you will eat your food until you return to the ground, since from it you were taken; for dust you are and to dust you will return." Adam was to live by the sweat of his brow from that point forth. And we've done that ever since.

The second place sweat is mentioned is Ezekiel 44:17–19, which tells us that the Levites and the priests were not supposed to wear garments that would cause them to sweat.

The third instance is in Luke 22:44, which describes a Man hugging the ground in the Garden while His followers sleep. He had come to do something about the sweat that comes to us as a result of being born on the wrong planet. It says, "And being in an agony he prayed more earnestly: and his sweat was as it were great drops of blood falling down to the ground" (KJV).

This Man is no middle-of-the-road moderate. He has come to pull out all the stops and live life at its ultimate as only God can do it, yet to live as a man and to discover what it's like to be here. Then He gives us a chance to get involved in the perspiration. God's goal for each of us is to do everything possible to become involved, or possibly more involved, in the work of the gospel.

The Bible continues to remind us that we are God's witnesses. The word shows up repeatedly (sixty-four times for *witness* and fifty for *witnesses*—more thrilling information).

It may turn some of us cold because we have this stereotype in our minds of what witness is. We think of it as someone who goes down the street and knocks at the doors of people he has never met before, hoping that no one answers. The alternative, an easier way that many of us have been exposed to, and what a wonderful escape it is, is to roll up papers into gospel bombs and drop them anonymously along country roads. Then you read *The Gospel Blimp,* that satire on the typical Christian stereotype of witness, and you realize what a comedy it really is.

Subsequently you begin to take a look at why a Christian witnesses anyway. Why did Jesus say, "Follow Me and I will make you fishers of men"? What did He have in mind? What is the purpose? And is the Christian life supposed to be easier, or is it supposed to be harder? If you check it out, you will find that the Scripture goes hot and cold on this point. In one place Jesus says, "If anyone would come after me, he must deny himself and take up his cross and follow me" (Matthew 16:24). Taking up your cross sounds like hard work. In another place He says, "Come to me, all you who are weary and burdened, and I will give you rest" (Matthew 11:28). That sounds like the opposite. Then you read in the writings of Paul, "work out your salvation with fear and trembling" (Philippians 2:12). Work at it, he admonishes. Then the same author says, "To the man who does not work but trusts God who justifies the wicked, his faith is credited as righteousness" (Romans 4:5). In Hebrews 4 he says that God invites us to rest. "Let us, therefore, make every effort [or "labor" in the KJV] to enter that rest" (Hebrews 4:11). Labor to enter into that rest—how do you do that? Have you ever labored to rest?

What is the work? And where does the sweat come in?

To begin with, I'd like to remind you of something that I have emphasized throughout my ministry, that the sweat doesn't earn my way to heaven. It does not mean paying for privileges or penance. Neither does the sweat involve trying to overcome sin and the devil. The down payment concerning the issues of righteousness and sin has already been taken care of and so have the monthly payments. Jesus paid it all. Not only in the beginning of the Christian life but every step of the way. It's all His work when it comes to sin and righteousness. This is a revolutionary idea to many of us who have thought that we have to work hard to live the Christian life.

There *is* work, and I would like to deny the charge that some have made against us, that we are Quietists, a Quaker strain of yesteryear who didn't believe in doing anything, because God does it all, so they just sat by the fire and rocked in a rocking chair. Maybe that is even going too far—you don't even rock, you just sit there. Don't pray if you don't feel like it. Don't eat a bite unless you feel like it. Don't get involved in service if you don't feel like it. There is where we go off the track, because there is work in the Christian life. There is sweat involved. This was Tim Hansel's point in his book *Holy Sweat*.

Here is the minicourse in the great experience of righteousness by faith. Text number one: John 15:5: "Without me you can do nothing." Text number two: Philippians 4:13: "We can do *all things* through Christ." Put the two together, and that is where the work comes. If without Him I can do nothing, but with Him I can do all things, then the effort and the work involved is in getting with Him. Does that take effort? If you haven't spent much time trying to get with Him or responding to His invitation to get with Him, perhaps you don't realize that there is effort involved. I believe that the Christian life takes every ounce of determination and grit and willpower and backbone and effort that we own toward what God has invited us to do and what He cannot do for us—the relationship. The relationship is based on three things. The first two are spending time with God on our knees day by day, reading His Word and communicating with Him in prayer. The third one—Christian service, witness, outreach, rolling up our sleeves and getting involved in the human race—is equally as important, and if we don't have the third one, the first two will go sour. As I mentioned before, it is a surprise for many people to discover that God gave us service and witness for our good. In fact, whatever necessity there is for our involvement in the work of God, He has purposely arranged it for our own sakes.

Can we have a part in someone being saved? Yes. Can we have a part in someone being lost? Yes. But the one who is going to be lost if I don't get involved in service and outreach is . . . guess who? Me, myself.

I'd like to invite you to look up a chapter in the book *The Desire of Ages*. It is chapter 70, titled " 'The Least of These My Brethren.' " This chapter has more information and insight per square inch of print than most anything around, and it has to do with this whole idea of service. The title of it is based on the verse, " ' "I tell you the truth, whatever you did for one of the least of these brothers of mine, you did for me" ' " (Matthew 25:40). Please read it carefully.

In the process of becoming involved in service and outreach, we discover what it means to take Jesus' yoke upon us and learn more of Him. And Jesus promises that if we do, we will discover that His yoke is easy and His burden is light. Does that mean there is no work involved in witness and service and outreach? No, there is a lot of sweat involved. But you will discover that it is harder work not to get involved. The person who doesn't get involved is the one who focuses on himself and becomes miserable. It always works that way. God knows the timeless principle: In helping others, we help ourselves more.

I've had a little problem differentiating between service and witness. While I was pastoring in southern California, we got into a discussion in one of our midweek meetings; and in the attempt to try and get rid of that terrible word *witness,* we threw out the baby with the bathwater. It appears that the word *service* has more to do with what we do and the word *witness* has to do with who we are and what we say. Our purpose for getting involved in service, in deeds of mercy, is that we might be effective in verbal witness, in giving testimonies to Jesus and His love. Not every person is going to find himself in the same shoes when it comes to method of service and method of witness. That's why we love to encourage individuals in finding their own creative ways of becoming more involved. Our purpose for service to others is that they will then be open to listen to the good news that we have to share of the wonderful Friend we find in Jesus.

How long has it been since you have thrilled to the idea of justification? Justification means standing before God, because of Jesus, as though we have never, ever sinned. Do you believe that? Can you accept the good news that because of Jesus you stand before God as though you have never sinned? That's available to you right now. Is that something worth telling someone about, sharing what a wonderful Friend we have in Jesus?

Many people won't be able to hear because they are too hungry. Many people won't be able to hear because they're lonely, or because they're cold or they're homeless or they're hurting. This is where we have a chance to combine service and witness. Thus, instead of one becoming an escape for the other, we have a combination that God had in mind all along.

There are different methods of service and witness. Paul describes the idea in Romans 12:4–7: "Just as each of us has one body with many members, and these members do not all have the same function, so in Christ we who are many form one body, and each member belongs to all the others. We have different gifts, according to the grace given us. If a man's gift is prophesying, let him use it in proportion to his faith." Everyone can do something.

One thing we know concerning Christian witness and service is this: It is not optional in the Christian life. It is not something that we take or leave. It is an absolute necessity. But the necessity turns into privilege when we realize Who we're working with. That's what takes all the sweat out of it.

My brother tried to walk to Los Angeles from Riverside in the fog one night, because he was in love. He put forth a lot of effort that night, but it would have been worse for him to stay home with his feet on the desk reading a book. That would have been harder work. He found that night that his yoke was easy and his burden light because he was in love. Is this not possible concerning what Jesus has done for us? Whether we call it duty or privilege, Christian service and witness are not optional in the Christian life. If we leave them out, our prayers will go sour. Our interest in the Bible will go bad. And we will end up focusing on ourselves and becoming miserable.

Here is a poem that some of us cut our teeth on.

There is a story I've been hearing
With a lesson that's most cheering,
And I'm sure that you would
Like to learn it too.

Well, a man was eating pastry,
And it must have been quite tasty,
When he thought of something
He would like to do.

He was sitting at the table,
Eating all that he was able,
When he spied a little ant upon the floor.

Placing the ant upon the pastry,
Which he thought had been quite tasty,
He was shocked to see the ant would eat no more.
Instead the ant left the table,
Ran as fast as he was able
Down the legs and raced across the floor.

So, the man gave close inspection
And he followed the direction
As he saw the ant rush through the open door.

On the street, the ant found others,
I don't know if friends or brothers,
But what he said just seemed to thrill them all.
Not a one made an indictment,
Every ant with great excitement,
Came and followed him in answer to his call.

They returned to the table,
Where they ate all they were able,
While the man stood by inspired.
By what he'd seen.
When he thought of all his neighbors,

And how circumscribed his labors,
He was shamed to be so selfish and so mean.

We believe the gospel story,
And we long for heaven's glory.
Let the world behold our hope to us is real.
And the message will go sweeter,
And our feet become much fleeter,
When we get the ants' evangelistic zeal.
—Adlai Albert Esteb

"Go to the ant, you sluggard; consider its ways and be wise!"
(Proverbs 6:6).

CHAPTER 7

INTERCESSORY PRAYER

A woman came to her pastor and asked if he would pray for the salvation of her husband. He said, "I'll make a deal with you. I will pray one hour a day for your husband if you will pray one hour a day for your husband." She thought for a moment and then said, "Well, never mind."

What would you do with that kind of agreement? Could you do it? Would you? Or is this asking too much?

What is the role of intercession in behalf of other people when it comes to prayer and the prayer life? The Bible has some pretty strong examples of intercession. Moses was probably one of the greatest. The Lord, through the prophet Isaiah, lamented the fact that there was no one interceding: "He saw that there was no one, he was appalled that there was no one to intervene" (Isaiah 59:16). There was no intercessor. When we think of intercession, of course, we think of Jesus. Isaiah 53:12 makes it clear that Jesus was a great intercessor: "Therefore I will give him a portion among the great, and he will divide the spoils with the strong, because he poured out his life unto death, and was numbered with the transgressors. For he bore the sin of many, and made intercession for the transgressors." And in Romans 8:26, we're told that the Holy Spirit is our Intercessor: "In the same way, the Spirit helps us in our weakness. We do not know what we ought to pray for, but the Spirit himself intercedes for us with groans that words cannot express." Also notice the good news in Hebrews 7:25: "Therefore he is able to save completely those who come to God through him, because he always lives to intercede for them." There's never a time when Jesus' intercession for created beings ceases. That's good news for some of us who thought for a long time that there would be a period when we would be without an intercessor.

God gives us the privilege of becoming involved in intercessory prayer, of becoming intercessors with Jesus. Perhaps we need to look at several reasons why. We're all familiar with the invitation that Jesus made, in Matthew 11:28, 29: " 'Come to me, all you who are weary and burdened, and I will give you rest. Take my yoke upon you and learn from me, for I am gentle and humble in heart, and you will find rest for your souls.' " We come to Him and find rest. This means that anyone who does not find the Christian life restful must not be coming to Jesus, because Jesus did not intend for the Christian life to be a heavy yoke.

Yet, in the middle of this passage, in verse 29, He says, " 'Take my yoke upon you and learn from me.' " This is very interesting because when we are invited to take His yoke upon us, this means that we are yoking up together with Him. That should not be a heavy yoke; it should rather be a privilege. You don't think you have enough strength to join? Well then, just rely upon His strength. Let Him pull you within the yoke. How could you ask for a better partner in the yoke than Jesus?

But it says also that the reason for yoking up with Him is to learn of Him, to get acquainted with Him, to find out more about Him. This is actually the way we grow in our Christian life. Our personal, private life with God is not going to get anywhere unless we yoke with Jesus in service. I'm convinced that in nine cases out of ten, the reason the Christian life goes sour and we lose the love we once had is that we fail to get involved in service and reaching out in witness with Christ. We do not get yoked up with Him. This is the way we learn about Him.

So, as far as God is concerned, His big reason for our involvement in service, in witness, in praying, in interceding, in becoming part of His intercession, is for our good. But that is not our reason for getting involved, or it would sound like a selfish reason. Our reason for getting involved is that if we have the real thing, a genuine life with God, we would not want to hold our peace; we will have something to share. The desire to share will come spontaneously. We don't have to figure out our motive, but we do know His motive. Whatever necessity there is for inviting us to become involved in the work of the gospel is for our good.

On the other hand, what does intercession not accomplish? We need to have this straight too so that we can be free to become involved with Him in His yoke.

Our witness to the gospel never determines anyone else's destiny. I have said that before, and I'm going to say it again, without all of the proof texts this time. Simply stated, you and I are not going to be responsible for anyone being saved or anyone being lost—not church members, not our children, not our family—nobody. If God is not big enough to give everyone an adequate opportunity concerning eternal life, He is not big enough to be God. We are not the only ones involved in service, not at all. In some of our big meetings, sometimes we give the impression that we are, but we're just a drop in the bucket.

All the heavenly resources are directed toward giving everyone born in this world an adequate opportunity for eternal life. This is based upon two premises. Number one: God is love. Number two: God is responsible for life. Therefore, He would not be a

God of love if He did not give everyone an adequate opportunity for something better regardless of what others do or don't do in the process.

This is brand new to many of our Adventist subculture, and it's not inherent in our mentality when we have spent years trying to make people feel guilty for not saving other people's lives, and teaching that others will be lost if we don't witness to them. I do not believe that at all. This takes the pressure off me and frees me to witness with complete peace, because if I'm not going to cause anyone to be lost by my mistakes, I can get involved in witness. I don't have to pay a dollar for the professionals to do it. I can do it myself and relax and enjoy. This is a concept that has flown right past us for a long time.

We have killed witness by trying to get people to witness from guilt. That's the way we've killed it, and we've done such a good job of killing witnessing that hardly 5 percent of church members get involved in any kind of organized witness or service.

However, our involvement, our prayers, our sharing, and our reaching out here and abroad can have an effect right now in terms of helping someone find out about the gospel sooner, or bringing peace to the troubled hearts that are fearful of the devil, or bringing hope to the heathen and the ignorant. We *can* make a difference.

Another encouraging thing is that we can have a part in someone's decision concerning their eternal destiny. We can have the joy someday of meeting them in the heavenly country, realizing we had a part in the decision they made. We can also have a part in freeing God to do what He would like to do—the things He won't do and can't do if we don't become involved.

In order to get a handle on what our prayers will accomplish to make a difference, we need to picture the heavenly courtroom scene. Jesus talked about it. The apostles talked about it. The courtroom scene includes the judge, the jury, the advocate, the defense—it's all there. Zechariah 3:1, 2 talks about the accuser standing ready to accuse Joshua the high priest. Revelation 12:10 speaks of the accuser of the brethren who was cast down by the cross of Jesus. We know who the prosecution is, and his name is spelled with a big D. We also know the Judge. God has committed all judgment to the Son. In 2 Timothy 4:8, Paul said in his famous speech, "Now there is in store for me the crown of righteousness, which the Lord, the righteous *Judge,* will award to me on that day—and not only to me, but also to all who have longed for his appearing" (emphasis added).

We also know who is our Advocate. It is interesting that Jesus is not only our Judge, He is also our Attorney. He says through the apostle John in 1 John 2:1, "My dear children, I write this to you so that you will not sin. But if anybody does sin, we have one who speaks to the Father in our defense—Jesus Christ, the Righteous One." The Bible is full of courtroom language. This gives us a clue as to why God can do things when we pray that He can't do if we don't pray.

All we have to do is look at the history of our own jurisprudence, which tells us that any judge or attorney who takes a case that is not appealed to him is overstepping his boundaries, especially when you have a prosecutor who is ready to shout "mistrial" or "no fair." And the enemy, the devil, is vicious on this.

We know that when the whole scene is over, at the end of the thousand years in heaven, when everybody who has ever lived or died meets for the first and last time, every knee will bow and every tongue will confess that Jesus Christ is Lord and that God has been fair. This includes the devil. God has bent over backwards for centuries to make sure the devil has no charge against Him in this great conflict. When the video replay on that three-hundred-sixty-degree big screen over the throne of God is finally finished and everyone who has been riveted to the movie version of the whole great controversy sees the beginning and the end, we understand that the devil himself will fall down on his knees and admit that God is fair and just, and that God has never overstepped Himself. This will be an impressive scene.

According to Scripture, then, it is possible for us to appeal our case to Him. Maybe this is the reason Jesus Himself was in the habit of praying out loud. I've been looking at that lately. When Jesus was praying out loud, the disciples came and found Him so absorbed in His out-loud praying that He didn't even notice them. They listened as He prayed out loud and His Father heard. Not only that, the enemy heard too. When you pray out loud, it seems, the enemy can hear things that he's not going to hear if you pray only in your mind. God can say, "Listen to that. Did you hear that? This case was appealed to Me. This case was brought before the heavenly court." The prosecutor has to back off and say, "Yes, it was."

In this heavenly court system, not only is it possible for me to appeal my case, it is possible for me to appeal the case of someone else who is not appealing his own case. Very interesting! It means that we can join God in the ministry of intercession and make a difference in His being able to do things at times when we pray that He can't if we don't pray.

One thing is very clear. God has bound Himself to proceed with His will as fast and as long as we join Him in freeing Him to do what He really wants to do by appealing case after case to the heavenly courtroom session.

With that in mind, let's look at a parable found in Luke, where we have a classic example of intercession.

> He said to them, "Suppose one of you has a friend, and he goes to him at midnight and says, 'Friend, lend me three loaves of bread, because a friend of mine on a

journey has come to me, and I have nothing to set before him.'

"Then the one inside answers, 'Don't bother me. The door is already locked, and my children are with me in bed. I can't get up and give you anything.' I tell you, though he will not get up and give him the bread because he is his friend, yet because of the man's boldness he will get up and give him as much as he needs" (Luke 11:5–8).

Then follows Jesus' famous statement, " 'Ask and it will be given to you; seek and you will find; knock and the door will be opened to you' " (Luke 11:9).

Notice that the friend in need is not in a life-threatening situation. He can get some bread tomorrow. He's not going to die tonight. So the issue here is not eternal destiny but rather the comfort and the needs of a friend. We see also that the one who needs bread and discovers that the 7-Eleven has already closed is *helpless* to meet the needs of the friend who has come to him.

What reason does the person in the story have for being bold to ask a friend? He remembers that his other friend has plenty and goes to ask a favor, not for himself but for another person. This noble act goes a lot deeper than "Please give me a new fire engine for Christmas, Santa Claus." This is more like, "Here is someone in need, and I'm going to get help for that needy person." When you're asking without a selfish motive, but rather trying to help someone else, you can be bold to ask for help.

My brother and his family came to visit while we lived in Colorado. One evening they watched my boy demonstrate how he had learned to put his head on one chair and his heels on another chair and lie straight across. My brother didn't think that his nephew should outsmart him, so he tried to do the same thing. In the process he threw his neck out.

The next day, my brother was in real agony. A member of our church was an orthopedic doctor, so I took my brother to him. The doctor was my friend, and in fact he had taken me canoeing on the river and had dumped me out of the canoe into the water. He really owed me one. But he was so busy that he didn't have time to see any new patients. I felt bold enough to go to him, however, because I wasn't asking for my own neck. I was asking for my brother's neck, and he made time.

The second thing, according to the Bible story, that made the person bold enough to ask was that he knew his friend had what was needed. And my doctor friend had what was needed. He took me into his office between patients and said, "Look, here's this machine that will contract your brother's muscles and his neck and shoulders. You can run it. I'll turn it on, and you run it." I was put in charge of running the machine and watching my brother's muscles contract. It got to be kind of fun, because this was a chance to get even with my brother for some past scores. I saw that the dial was only on three, so I cranked it up to nine. When I got up near the base of his skull, he said, "Oh, keep going. I just got a bunch of new sermon ideas."

My friend was willing to help me because he was my friend. When the person in the Bible story goes to get help from his friend, he already has a relationship established. This is relationship theology.

Here is the third reason you can afford to be bold with your friend. The Scripture presents it in a rather interesting way. "I tell you, though he will not get up and give him the bread *because he is his friend*" (Luke 11:8). Because they were friends, he said, "No, I can't help you now." Only friends can talk that way. If you went to the pastor at midnight and said, "Look, I need some help for someone who has come to visit," and the pastor didn't know you very well, he would probably try to put his best foot forward and play the right role. But if you are his friend he can say, "Go away! I'm not going to help you right now."

But the man in the story hung in there, and he was bold about it because they were friends, because he was asking for another, and because he knew that this person had the kind of help they needed. He stayed with it. This is a mighty illustration in Jesus' own language of what it means to go to bat for someone else— intercession.

Again we are not talking about eternal life. There are a lot of things this side of eternal life for which our prayers can make a difference. You could list all kinds of needs about which God is freed to act because of our intercession, in a way that He would not be freed to move if we didn't. The great controversy is being conducted by an all-wise God who is determined that no one will ever shout, "Mistrial." What an awesome privilege it is to be involved with God in intercession.

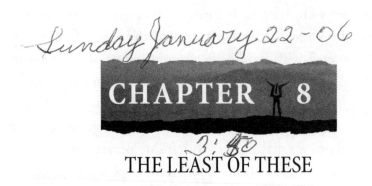

Sunday January 22-06

CHAPTER 8

3:50

THE LEAST OF THESE

I was debating with myself one time, after coming back from a long trip, what to talk about for church service. We had planned a series on prayer, and after going through all the prayers of the Bible, I discovered to my surprise that there are only a handful of group prayers. All the rest of them have to do with individuals praying for something or someone.

I got interested in studying Acts 4 on group prayer, where they were praying for the disciples, but thought better of that. Then I considered 2 Chronicles 20 on Jehoshaphat and the call to prayer with his group. I considered talking about the rich fool but got the victory over that one. I also considered talking about Peter, of whom Jesus said, "I have prayed for you."

When I got to my office that week and looked at my desk, I discovered a letter. This letter deeply moved me and became the basis of what I talked about that Sabbath morning. It said,

Dear Pastor Venden,
I sat through the young adult class on Sabbath, but I could not really concentrate. Things are tight around my

house. I knew I had no money to buy groceries this week. The kids were going back to school, and I wasn't sure how I was going to feed them. I looked around the [Sabbath School] room and saw a lot of grocery bags like somebody had just come from Stater Brothers [grocery store]. As I saw the boxes of Cheerios, I thought, if I can only have one of those, then we could eat breakfast until payday. At the end of the second service I went and asked who this food was for, and they said Azure Hills [church] has a food bank. I wondered what that was. They sent me to a different place to ask someone there. They had me fill out a card and then they gave me a shopping list to fill in.

My hand was shaking and I felt like screaming and crying at the same time. But, decided to do that later. We came home with a load to hold us for a long time. My kids were so excited because they know how tough things have been lately. We placed the food on the table, and we all knelt down by it and thanked God who said, I will not leave you nor forsake you.

Then we all screamed and we cried. Our situation will improve, God willing, in a couple years. But, I will never forget Saturday, August 27, 1995, when the heavens were open and food came to our house via the angels at my own church.

Whoever these people are, please, please thank them for us. Thank them for taking time to think of someone going through hard times. Thank them for sharing the blessings that they have received from above. Thank them for our kids who had Sabbath dinner that day with ramen soup. Santa Claus could not have brought the same joy. It doesn't really matter who I am. But, when Jesus comes, I know He will look into the faces of those who volunteered and who gave dollars. And He will say, "Thanks for taking care of one of the least of these my brethren."

Things weren't always this way at our household. Things change sometimes with no warning. Today it was us. Tomorrow, God willing, when we are back on our feet again, we will be able to help someone else. Thanks.

—A member of the Azure Hills Church for ten years.

I decided to take all of my money for the building fund and give it to the food bank. But then I got the victory over that one too. I'm not here trying to promote a social gospel in which we neglect devotions and relationship with Jesus and replace it with helping those less fortunate. I'm not interested in the social gospel that has caused people to make *it* the entire plan of becoming growing Christians. But Jesus had something to say about this in Matthew 25:31–40:

"When the Son of Man comes in his glory, and all the angels with him, he will sit on his throne in heavenly glory. All the nations will be gathered before him, and he will separate the people one from another as a shepherd separates the sheep from the goats. He will put the sheep on his right and the goats on his left.

"Then the King will say to those on his right, 'Come, you who are blessed by my Father; take your inheritance, the kingdom prepared for you since the creation of the world. For I was hungry and you gave me something to eat, I was thirsty and you gave me something to drink, I was a stranger and you invited me in, I needed clothes and you clothed me, I was sick and you looked after me, I was in prison and you came to visit me.'

"Then the righteous will answer him, 'Lord, when did we see you hungry and feed you, or thirsty and give you something to drink? When did we see you a stranger and invite you in, or needing clothes and clothe you? When did we see you sick or in prison and go to visit you?'

"The King will reply, 'I tell you the truth, whatever you did for one of the least of these brothers of mine, you did for me.' "

How long has it been since you got shaken out of your own little comfortable circle and came to the realization that someone would really be happy for a box of Cheerios? I guess I had forgotten about borrowing nickels and dimes out of our kids' piggy banks when they were small so that we could go and get another quart of milk. But the letter brought back those memories. Maybe Conrad Hilton was right in his autobiography when he said that he needed to remember what it was like to be a pauper twenty years before he paid cash for the Waldorf Astoria hotel. Most people, even the most wealthy, have had some interesting times of being in want, and Jesus addressed this.

An interesting commentary on this scripture appears in *The Desire of Ages,* the classic book on the life of Christ. It starts out with a rather breathtaking premise. In fact, if that's all we read, we might question it.

"Christ on the Mount of Olives pictured to His disciples the scene of the great judgment day. And He represented its decision as turning upon one point. When the nations are gathered before Him, there will be but two classes, and their eternal destiny will be determined by what they have done or have neglected to do for Him in the person of the poor and the suffering" (637).

It sounds like setting the stage for salvation by works, salvation by social gospel, or salvation by running the food bank. It even gets a little heavier: "In that day Christ does not present before men the great work He has done for them in giving His life for their redemption. He presents the faithful work they have done for Him" (ibid).

I had to read the rest of the chapter to find out the principle: No one gets to heaven by helping the poor or those less fortunate. But those who have accepted God's grace and are in a continuing relationship with Jesus begin to have a heart that beats the same with His heart. It is a heart that cares. It cares so much that He went on a long journey from heaven to earth into our station. He couldn't have gone any lower. And now He invites us to consider those who are less fortunate than we are.

There is definite evidence that a person has accepted salvation in how they treat those less fortunate. In fact even the heathen, we are told, who exhibit kindness but have never heard the story of the Cross and the gospel, have actually been worked upon by the Holy Spirit, and their actions are an evidence of God's involvement in their lives. We have noticed earlier this comment concerning them.

> Those whom Christ commends in the judgment may have known little of theology, but they have cherished His principles. Through the influence of the divine Spirit they have been a blessing to those about them. Even among the heathen are those who have cherished the spirit of kindness. . . . Among the heathen are those who worship God ignorantly, those to whom the light is never brought by human instrumentality, yet they will not perish. . . . Their works are evidence that the Holy Spirit has touched their hearts, and they are recognized as the children of God (*The Desire of Ages*, 638).

As I pondered this comment on the Scripture, I thought that we should go out and help our brothers, help our sisters, help those in the church, the family of God. Don't let anyone go without Cheerios. And to my surprise, I was invited to go into a further outreach, to a whole world gone wrong, and to be interested in reaching out and helping the fallen, the erring, the sinful, the prisoners— not the prisoners who are jailed simply because of love for Jesus, but the vile, the carnal, the corrupt. After all, isn't this what Jesus did when He came on His long journey to the planet that we were born on? If Jesus has an equal care for all the souls that He has created, and if our hearts are beating in unison with His, shouldn't it make us want to go out and help? Particularly if we have our eyes open and aren't bound by the little circle that we operate in day by day. We must not forget there are some people who don't have any Cheerios.

How does heaven look at this world of struggling poor people? "Angels of heaven are passing throughout the length and breadth of the earth, seeking to comfort the sorrowing, to protect the imperiled, to win the hearts of men to Christ. Not one is neglected or passed by. God is no respecter of persons, and He has an equal care for all the souls He has created" (*The Desire of Ages,* 639).

So, maybe it was an angel who had something to do with guiding the person to the right place so that the kids could have something to eat again.

All heaven is involved in the work of the gospel and the plan of salvation, millions and millions of intelligent beings. We might ask ourselves, if no one is neglected or passed by and they are not going to perish even if they don't hear the good news of the gospel from *us,* then why can't we sit by the fireside and eat apples and popcorn? We have forgotten that the most miserable people are the ones who move in their own circle, concerned about their own things and not caring about the things of others.

We used to go to Disneyland, but we quit going. It went sour when my conservative parents were there. We thought the Matterhorn looked like a scenic little ride. We didn't realize it was a roller coaster until my parents were going up. My mother made promises to God. My daughter got mad at me, because she thought I was driving. But the reason we decided we weren't going back anymore was the children were always grumpy and grouchy afterward on the way home. If you have just experienced the greatest vegetarian entertainment in the world and you have no place to go but down, all you can do is be grumpy and grouchy on the way home.

"Oh," they begged, "we want to go again."

"No, we're not going again. You're grumpy on the way home."

"We promise we won't be grumpy." But they always were.

Then the day came when I decided to take my daughter to visit the nursing home with me. She wanted to go. To my surprise she discovered that she had a heart for people who were lonely or hurting. She gave them a smile and a pat, and she talked and listened. She told me, "Bye, Dad. I'll meet you in the lobby." And down the hall she went to visit as many as she could. I couldn't understand it. But I did understand this much. On the way home there was no griping or grumpiness. She was happy. Does that ring any bells? We don't have to spend our time wondering whether we're going to get to heaven or face the Judgment Day. All we have to do is realize that God is interested in our happiness. And the one who reaches out and helps others is the one who is going to be the happiest.

Many feel that it would be a great privilege to visit the scenes of Christ's life on earth, to walk where He trod, to look upon the lake beside which He loved to teach, and the hills and valleys on which His eyes so often rested. But we need not go to Nazareth, to Capernaum, or to Bethany, in order to walk in the steps of Jesus. We shall find His footprints beside the sickbed, in the hovels of poverty, in the crowded alleys of the great city, and in every place where there are human hearts in need of consolation. In doing as Jesus did when on earth, we shall walk in His steps (*The Desire of Ages*, 640).

In doing as Jesus did when He was on earth, we shall walk in His footsteps. That's the quickest and the best way yet to the Holy Land. When we don't get involved in helping those less fortunate, we remain at the ABCs stage of Christian experience. If we want to grow, we reach out, and if we don't, the sequel is rather serious.

"In the great judgment day those who have not worked for Christ, those who have drifted along, carrying no responsibility, thinking of themselves, pleasing themselves, will be placed by the Judge of all the earth with those who did evil. They receive the same condemnation" (*Christ's Object Lessons*, 365).

Jesus feels very deeply about this question.

You don't have to be poor in financial things to be in need. Some people may be rich in money and be starving because of a background that left them bruised and battered. They didn't have the advantage that you had, so they don't know how to love or be loved. Someone might be rich when it comes to resources but not be able to have the faith to get hold of the good news. You can reach out to them as well. Let's not just confine it to the financial picture. And reaching out as the angels of heaven do is a privilege, not a duty. It will have tremendous results in how we live and how we feel.

For instance, are you worried about the restless energy of your teenagers? My father used to worry about that. He had two bad boys growing up into teenagers. We lived in Modesto, and he got a place out in the outskirts where we could dig holes and fill them in again. We could take down the picket fence and make twice as many pickets and nail them back on and paint it and paint it and paint it, because he wanted to keep us off the streets. He was worried about the restless energy of his teenagers. But listen to this: The restless energy that is so often a source of danger to the young might be directed into channels through which it would flow out in streams of blessing. Self would be forgotten in earnest work to do others good.

Those who minister to others will be ministered unto by the Chief Shepherd. They themselves will drink of the living water, and will be satisfied. [Satisfied!] They will not be longing for exciting amusements, or for some change in their lives (*The Desire of Ages,* 640, 641).

Wow! Why do we long for exciting amusement? We're looking for something for ourselves—a selfish thrill.

I've met people again and again who have said, "I don't understand how this Christian life works. It has never done anything for me. I've been a Christian for twenty years and I'm the same as I was before. The only thing I ever overcame was chewing my fingernails. When is it going to change?" I have experienced this myself. It got my attention the day I read that sentence. "Those who minister to others . . . will not be longing for some change in their lives." This addresses the restless youth. It addresses the miserable person. And it addresses the one who is looking for something satisfying.

How wonderful it is to realize such a simple answer. Our only solution is to go to our knees and pray the higher prayer found in the hymn book. Have you pondered this lately?

At first I prayed for light:
Could I but see the way,

How gladly, swiftly would I walk
To everlasting day!

And next I prayed for strength:
That I might tread the road
With firm unfaltering feet, and win
The heaven's serene abode.

And then I asked for faith:
Could I but trust my God,
I'd live infolded in His peace,
Though foes were all abroad.

But now I pray for love:
Deep love to God and man;
A living love that will not fail,
However dark His plan.

And light and strength and faith
Are opening everywhere!
God waited patiently until
I prayed the larger prayer.[1]

Love is the larger prayer! Love for people who may seem inferior and less fortunate, just as Jesus prayed for them.

Two students went abroad for a year to study in Collonges, France. During that year, they had three vacation times when they could go out and do the tourist thing. The two young men made plans to travel on the train to Paris for their first time off. But things went bad and got worse. They lost their tickets. They lost their passports. They lost their money. They were finally happy to crawl back to Collonges to sit it out for the rest of the vacation.

The second vacation period came and they said, "We're not going to the tourist traps. We're going to get a motor scooter and ride the back country and meet the peasants." So they got on a motor scooter with their sleeping bags, and things went bad. The motor scooter burned up. The tires went flat, and the sleeping bags got moldy after lying in the mud in the vineyard in the rain. Finally, they were happy to get back to Collonges to sit out the rest of the vacation.

The third vacation time came. They said, "We better not do anything this time." Except they had one thought. They put their toothbrushes in their back pockets, and they started walking down the hill and through the forest to see if they could find someone who needed help.

Midday they came to a clearing where there was an old, dilapidated cabin where a hermit-type man lived. He was grumpy and grouchy. They tried to talk with him using the little French they knew and some sign language, and they found out he lived alone. His family was gone—all dead. He was just waiting to die. The place was a shambles, with doors hanging on broken hinges and chickens running in and out of the cabin. The boys got permission to work. They cleaned the outside of the cabin. They moved into the inside and scrubbed the floors and washed the windows. That night they got dinner for the old man, who showed them the table cloth that was one of his wife's favorites. They sat around the table that evening, and there was new light in the man's darkened world. They stayed the night. The next morning they bid him goodbye, leaving the grumpy man with a big smile on his face and sunshine in his heart. And they went on their way to find someone else to help.

Midday they found a group of peasants trying frantically to get the hay in. It was going to rain, and they weren't going to make it. The boys yelled for pitchforks, and they began to pitch hay. They pitched hay all afternoon until just before dark, and then the rain came. The hay was all in. And they sat with a happy family around a simple meal of soup and bread. That night they slept in the hay mound while the rain beat on the roof. They were never so tired in their lives, but they were never so happy.

When I heard these two boys tell the story of the rest of their vacation, when all they did was work hard trying to help someone else, I was moved because they said it was the best vacation they ever had. What fools we mortals are! We seek our own happiness, when the truth is that "he who now will bless the poor shall himself find blessing." I pray that God will give us the broader look and lead us to those who need us.

---

[1] "At First I Prayed for Light." Mrs. E. D. Cheney / C. E. Kettle. *Seventh-day Adventist Hymnal,* #488. Review and Herald Publishing Association, 1985.

Monday January 23-06

CHAPTER ⚹ 9

THE WOMAN AT THE WELL, PART I

I hope you have learned to ponder the Scripture with the idea of finding yourself in the picture. Bill Gaither has told thousands that this is a meaningful way to study the Bible. Read it as though you were there. Find yourself in the picture. Let's join the woman at the well. Her story is found in John 4 and contains enough for a whole book by itself. We'll have an overview of the story in this chapter.

"Now he [Jesus] had to go through Samaria. So he came to a town in Samaria called Sychar, near the plot of ground Jacob had given to his son Joseph. Jacob's well was there" (John 4:4–6).

Jacob's well is still there. I stood there one time, underneath a church. (They build a church over everything in the Holy Land now, except the Sea of Galilee.) Down in the basement of this church you can see Jacob's well, probably the closest thing to authenticity that you can still find today. It still goes down over a hundred feet, and if you want to use the same cup that millions of others have used, you can have a drink. Some of us chose not to. But there was the well that Jacob had dug, even though there was plenty of water everywhere—springs and fountains. He dug it because of some sort of dispute among land-owners.

Jesus comes to this well, and "tired as he was from the journey, sat down by the well. It was about the sixth hour" (John 4:6). It was around noon, and Jesus was weary. That's novel, isn't it? God tired? He was still God, but Jesus did not come to live as God. He came to live as a man, as a human being. That is good news for the human race.

He was more tired than the rest of the disciples, it seems, because they went into town to buy food, but Jesus, exhausted, stayed behind. Perhaps he had had one of those days that began long before dawn, when He responded to the call of the Holy Spirit to be out alone to spend time with His Father and to understand what it meant to have a fresh baptism of the Holy Spirit that day. Yet maybe that had nothing to do with His being tired because when you have the experience of the special anointing of the Holy Spirit, it brings energy. Perhaps He was tired and weary because He had been working with people and virtue had gone out of Him, as it is expressed at times in other stories. Or perhaps this day was hot and dusty. At any rate, Jesus was sitting at the well alone, weary and thirsty.

"When a Samaritan woman came to draw water, Jesus said to her, 'Will you give me a drink?' " (John 4:7). Here is a master at work when it comes to Christian service and witness. If you like to find how to better share whatever you want to share, you follow Jesus' method. You don't offer a favor, you ask for one. It's interesting that when you ask a favor of someone, a degree of trust is developed. Have you experienced that? And when Jesus asked for a drink of water, it wasn't long before He was asked for a drink of water.

Some people are disenchanted with the old method of organized witness, in which everyone goes down the streets ringing doorbells of people they have never met before. And some people today are so disenchanted with the old routine words and methods that they would like to explore witnessing as a way of life. We are way overdue on that. We need the kind of witness that goes on all through the day with the people we rub shoulders with at work, on the streets. But we don't know how to do it. For people who don't know how to witness or how to get started, asking a favor is a good place to start.

I discovered when I was in school on a college campus that it didn't work to try telling someone about my faith, what little I felt I had. But it did work to ask someone to tell me about their faith. That was one of the most meaningful things I ever did, asking someone how they became a Christian. I asked them, "Why are you on this Christian campus? Would you mind telling me?" I found out that they wanted to talk about it, but they weren't going to choke someone else with it. They were delighted to be asked.

So we see Jesus beginning this soul-winning adventure by simply requesting a drink of water. "The Samaritan woman said to him, 'You are a Jew and I am a Samaritan woman. How can you ask me for a drink?' (For Jews do not associate with Samaritans.)" (John 4:9). Of course, what else is new? We know that the Samaritans were considered heathens and dogs. Jews and Samaritans had been enemies for years. And there is something else interesting about this story. Jesus was talking to a woman, and if you study the low regard with which women were held in those days, you realize how exceedingly significant this is.

Something else that comes into the picture here is that she was not only just a woman, but not the head of the city council in the little village nearby, not even on the home and school board or parent-teacher association. She had to go out of town two-thirds of a mile to the well that Jacob had dug probably because she was *persona non grata* down at the town well where the women gathered. The gossip ran high. The people evaluated religion, God, faith, and eternity in terms of behavior in those days, and five husbands did not recommend her in that culture. Living with one who was not her husband didn't help either. So here we have a Samaritan dog, a heathen, someone considered to be of the lower gender, one that was considered a terrible sinner, and Jesus opens the conversation. No wonder the disciples were surprised when they came back.

She too wondered aloud. "Why do you ask me for a drink?"

"Jesus answered her, 'If you knew the gift of God and who it is that asks you for a drink, you would have asked him and he would have given you living water' " (John 4:10). Notice that Jesus said, "If you knew the *gift* of God." Here we have a society of people, along with the ones in Jerusalem, who were victims of the system of religion that has always plagued us and still does today with the idea that you earn what you get and get what you earn. You've got to work for salvation. It's not a gift. You have to put your time in. It's righteousness by muscle. It is entering the city of God after putting forth lots of effort to keep those commandments, including the traditions. But Jesus says, "If you knew the gift of God." I'd like to invite you to sit down someday and go through your Bible and check out all the things that are gifts.

But here we're not talking primarily of the other things that are gifts, such as repentance, forgiveness, justification, peace, and all the rest of them. What we're talking about here is the One indicated in the third chapter of John: "For God so loved the world that he *gave* his one and only Son, that whoever believes in him shall not perish but have eternal life." We're not talking about the "what." We're not talking about philosophy or theology, as helpful as that can be. We're talking about THE GIFT. Again, "If you knew the gift of God and who it is that asks you for a drink," He is the Gift. Jesus has come on a long, expensive journey to help people understand that He is on the gift system. All we can do is receive the gift, and the way we receive the gift is to receive Him. He brings all the other gifts that God has to offer with Him.

I'd like to propose that this is the biggest problem in the Christian church. It's the biggest problem in all world religions, and it has permeated the Christian church as well. We don't know how to receive a gift. We don't want to receive a gift. Somewhere along the line of understanding salvation and the gospel, we have to weave our own efforts in and get some credit. When we discover that we cannot get any credit for our own efforts toward working our own way in, that *our* ways, whether they are subtle or more open, are futile, thousands of us will walk away from it. The greatest, most worldwide religion that professes Christianity has as its basis giving people something to do to make it with God. And this is not simply confined to some throne over in Europe, by any means.

Of all the materials written during 1988 to mark the centennial year of the famous 1888 General Conference session, to me the greatest (head and shoulders above all of the theology and all of the scholarly works), was a simple statement of the problem with grace by Deborah Anfenson-Vance, titled "The Trouble With Grace, a Tough Truth for Nice People."

> Grace can be a problem. The Bible, in fact, brims with unsettling stories that show how grace, again and again, upsets the apple cart as we know it.
>
> Big brother stews when Dad throws a party for a money-grubbing runaway who, down on his luck, has come home.
>
> Full-time employees grumble when the boss pays all his part-time workers a whole day's wage.
>
> Ninety-nine sheep are left at risk while a shepherd searches for one that is lost.
>
> Now I might find these stories funny, even useful, if I

happened to be the runaway son, the part-time worker, or one lost sheep. But a high-achieving, denominationally educated, church-employed, fourth-generation church member can hardly be typified in such terms. There's too much of that old-time religion coursing through my conscientious good-kid veins.

So, I catch myself sympathizing with the elder brother, the full-time worker, and the ninety and nine even though I've heard these stories seventy times seven times and know the punch lines like Mother's voice. . . . Grace seems against me, and I am not amused.

Good people, who take these stories seriously, may see that part of the trouble with grace is that it doesn't take good people seriously. At least not as seriously as we take ourselves.

For some years now, I have prided myself in not being a legalist, whatever that is. The trouble with grace is that it doesn't leave room for me to get uppity about anything I am or am not, and it's pretty much blind to the names I call myself. Which brings me to another point.

Grace is troublesome not only to the legalist or religious person. Grace can be tough stuff even for ordinary, nice people to stomach. And if you want to go one further, I will say this: there is something about human nature in general that makes it hard for any of us to hold out an empty hand. Because if we did, grace would fill that hand. And what could be more troublesome than that?

Gifts are a problem to us. We are disciples of the make-your-own-way, the pull-your-own-weight system. We are capable, self-reliant, high-achieving. And we are guilty. We believe, deep down, that we don't deserve anything we haven't worked, suffered, or paid for, and we narrow our eyes at the free-lunch crowd. For all our talk about giving, more often than not, we mix the reality with trade and obligation; it embarrasses us to take a gift when we have no way of paying it back.

Accepting an out-and-out gift is tantamount to charity, which, from childhood, nice people learn is good to give and bad to take. But if polite people have difficulty taking grace as the gift that it is, we also have trouble with the way it turns our good order on its head. We believe in white hats and black hats, and we don't like the way grace seems to mix them up and, more often than not, let the wrong hat ride off with the princess into the sunset, while Mr. Deserving stands sniffling alone at the unfairness of it all. There is something untamed about a God who would sponsor that sort of end to the show. It is obvious we have not yet successfully civilized Him to our sense of justice and propriety.

I could mention many more problems that grace poses, but I'm going to stop here and go instead to another story Jesus told. Even Jesus admitted that grace could be problematic. . . .

And here is the story:

"No one sews a patch of unshrunk cloth on an old garment, for the patch will pull away from the garment, making the tear worse. [You cannot mix righteousness by faith and righteousness by works.] Neither do men pour new wine into old wineskins. If they do, the skins will burst, the wine will run out and the wineskins will be ruined. No, they pour new wine into new wineskins, and both are preserved" (Matthew 9:16, 17, NIV).

I have to be a new creature in order to understand and appreciate the Gospel, otherwise it will destroy me.

So, in the meeting of old and new, we may recognize that the trouble with grace is the trouble with us. We are old shirts for new cloth, old vessels for new wine . . . too proud for the gift.

But grace also comes to elder brothers, and with it a choice. We may hold tight to life as *we* think it should be, cling to what makes *us* believe we are good, and do what makes sense to *our* vision—and has all along.

Or we can follow the hard and apparently senseless words: "Whoever tries to keep his life will lose it, and whoever loses his life will preserve it" (Luke 17:33, NIV) and open ourselves to grace, believing it will give us something beyond the shredded rags and the burst containers, though we haven't the foggiest idea what that will be.

And I, myself, cannot say what that will be, because it is the nature of grace to surprise. And for the rest of our lives, every time we think we've unwrapped the last package and walked through the last door, and are about to ask What more could there possibly be? We will find some thing to open sitting at our feet and something to walk through standing in front of us.

One more thing I can say: We who let go of our righteousness and lose our lives will gain a new view of those unsettling stories. We will see ourselves lost in a herd of ninety and nine, as a prodigal in our elder brotherliness, and as chronically late to our full-time jobs. Then we may know a Shepherd, a Father, a generous Boss. We may find our lives and laugh at the unexpectedness of it all.

For as surely as we know ourselves lost, we shall be found. Found by a grace whose business is not to make good folks better but to search out wandering ones and take them home. Take them home to a party.

I would like to suggest that when all of this is said and done that the problem they had in 1888 and 1988, the problem we have in the twenty-first century is the same problem as in the days of Jesus. We have a hard time understanding that "the wages of sin is death. But the gift of God is eternal life." I can accept the truth that I don't have to work and earn God's favor in terms of pardon and acceptance and still work hard to do what *He* would like to do in changing my life. I can accept the good news that the Lamb of God is sufficient, that Jesus paid it all at the cross, and still be trying to work my way to the Promised Land, or in some way put forth the proper amount of effort to be able to come up to the gates of the city and say, "I have the right to the tree of life." We cannot mix the old and the new, unless we admit the error that the faith gospel is supposed to uproot. We will be new wine in old wineskins and new cloth on old cloth. It does not work.

And so Jesus said, "If you knew the gift of God and who it is that asks you for a drink, you would have asked him and he would have given you living water" (John 4:10).

" 'Sir,' the woman said, 'you have nothing to draw with and the well is deep. Where can you get this living water?' " (John 4:11). The water is deep. Yes, the human systems, the human methods of trying to find refreshment and life, often seem deep. This is one of the things that perturbed the religious leaders in the days of Jesus about His method and His style of teaching and preaching. It was too simple. They wanted to ask something that the scholars would go to the head of the class with. We have made the well too deep. I think even the apostle Paul did it, although he couldn't help it. Jesus made it simple. And this really burned them, that it could be so simple that boys and girls could understand it. Jesus said, "Feed My sheep." Not my giraffes. And I'm glad when I hear someone say that if you feed the sheep, whatever the sheep can get, the giraffes can also get if they get down low enough.

The well is deep. "Are you greater than our father Jacob, who gave us the well and drank from it himself, as did also his sons and his flocks and herds?" (John 4:12). Appeal to the fathers, if you please. What was good enough for Father was good enough for me. The woman was saying, don't tell me that you have something greater than what came from the fathers. Of course this has always been a problem in religion. It's a surprise to discover that God has no grandsons. I used to think I could slide into heaven on my preacher father's coattail, and then I discovered that God has no grandsons or granddaughters. We have all kinds of ways of trying to slide into the heavenly kingdom. My wife confessed to me shortly after we were married that that is one reason she wanted to marry a preacher, to be able to slide into heaven on his coattail. It didn't take her long to get that out of her system. What was good enough for Grandpa was good enough for me, and this is the very reason why we have three or four hundred different denominations today. But the woman at the well didn't realize that she was talking to someone who was greater than her father Jacob.

"Jesus answered, 'Everyone who drinks this water will be thirsty again' " (John 4:13). Think of all the ways that people try to find satisfaction and the thirst still persists. I can still hear that temperance leader of yesteryear who stood up in front of the youth at camp meeting and said, "Chesterfields. They satisfy. No, they don't." He said, "I know a man who started smoking one pack a day. He wasn't satisfied. He increased it to two packs a day. He still wasn't satisfied. Three packs a day." And so it goes with whatever the scene is—drugs or other pleasures. People stumble over themselves to Monte Carlo and Reno and Vegas with this horrible sense that whoever drinks of this water is going to thirst again and again and again.

" 'But whoever drinks the water I give him will never thirst. Indeed, the water I give him will become in him a spring of water welling up to eternal life' " (John 4:14). Have you tasted of that? Are you interested? I'm interested. Jesus stood up at the feast of those religious people and in a loud voice He gave them the good news. " 'If anyone is thirsty, let him come to me and drink' " (John 7:37). He doesn't mean that one sip will suffice. He means that if we once taste of it, we will want to continue to taste of the unending supply. It knows no end, and it's the only thing that brings satisfaction.

The water of life sounds nebulous, ethereal, unreal, like Ponce de Leon in Florida looking for the evasive Fountain of Youth, or chasing the end of the rainbow. But it is just as simple as Jesus' own talk. Taking the water of life is sitting down with His Word through whom the Holy Spirit works and reading the stories from long ago that tell us what Jesus told the woman at the well.

I thank God that He made provision for us to never thirst again. I thank Him that we can leave our water pots at the earthly cisterns and join that woman of long ago, who was looked upon kindly by the Lord of heaven. I would like to take courage today concerning the Gift, and I would like to know the Gift, whom to know is life eternal. Wouldn't you?

CHAPTER 10

THE WOMAN AT THE WELL, PART II

There are three death sports, as they are commonly known among sports people: skydiving, scuba diving, and rock climbing. Rock climbing invaded our family with a teenage son, who, when he went on to college, wanted to do the bigger ones. His mother prayed for a broken leg before it became more severe.

One time my son was climbing Middle Cathedral, opposite El Capitan in Yosemite National Park. With him was a physician from Modesto. It was a two-day climb, and they were to sleep out overnight hanging in ropes on the sheer rock, twice as high above the ground as the World Trade Center in New York.

They made some serious blunders. On the first day, they dropped the canteen and a camera, and dehydration set in. The next day, when they finally made it over the top of the rock, the doctor, who was a little older and more wasted, lying on his face, moaned, "Water. Get water. Money is no problem. Just get water!" My son stumbled and crawled his way to a creek and buried his face in the water then managed to get some back to the doctor. They discovered, to their surprise, that they had lost twenty pounds on the climb. They were fortunate to come out alive.

As the song says,
> Water, pure water that sparkles so bright
> Beautiful, fresh, and free.

We don't realize what it's like until it's gone. Water is what makes you thirsty when the well is dry.

I remember when I was in the Middle East with Elder H. M. S. Richards, Sr., on his last Holy Land tour, and we were in Upper Egypt, where clear water was at a premium. My precious water bottle dropped on the floor in the airport in Upper Egypt, and I found myself exclaiming impulsively, "My water just broke!" I never heard the end of that one. If you travel overseas in some countries where you're frightened to death of the revenge of their particular system, water is something you cry for. You say, "Give me water, or I die." That's why the story of the woman at the well, which we began in the last chapter, is something that comes to life when you consider your own experience of seeking water.

In the last chapter we noticed that Jesus asked the Samaritan woman a favor and that it wasn't long before she asked Him for a favor. After she had asked why a Jew like Him would ask water of her, a Samaritan, He said, "If you knew the *gift of God* and who it is that asks you for a drink, you would have asked him and he would have given you living water" (John 4:10). This is one of the major keys in this story. Salvation is a gift, and we are not used to that. Instead we have our merit system. So this is the first thing we want to nail down in this chapter. We're not used to it being a gift, and that's why we make our Pathfinders ride their bicycles for half a day in order to get money. We have our marathons, and we have our humanistic ways of raising money and doing the work of the church, the same kinds of ways that IBM and Coca Cola use. But they are not God's ways.

One of the churches I was pastoring advertised that the church was offering free memberships for a month. Well, that's true, memberships are free. But salvation, even though it's free, still costs us everything. How do we understand that?

Here is something from a godly preacher south of the border, Juan Carlos Ortiz, who said rather effectively,

> Jesus said in Matthew 13 that the Kingdom of God was like a merchant looking for pearls. And when he found the pearl of great price, he sold everything he had to buy it.
>
> Of course, some Christians think the story means, we are the pearl of great price and Christ had to give up everything to redeem us. But now we understand that *He* is the pearl of great price. We are the merchants seeking for happiness, for security, for fame, for eternity.
>
> And when we find Jesus, it costs us everything. He has happiness, joy, peace, healing, security, eternity, everything." So we say, "I want this pearl. How much is it?"
>
> "Well," the seller says, "it's very expensive."
>
> "But how much?" we ask.
>
> "Well, a very large amount."
>
> "Do you think I could buy it?"
>
> "Oh, of course, everyone can buy it."
>
> "But didn't you say it was very expensive?"
>
> "Yes."
>
> "Well, how much is it?"
>
> "Everything you have," says the seller.
>
> We make up our minds. "All right, I'll buy it," we say.
>
> "Well, what do you have?" he wants to know. "Let's write it down."
>
> "Well, I have ten thousand dollars in the bank."
>
> "Good—ten thousand dollars. What else?"
>
> "That's all. That's all I have."

"Nothing more?"

"Well, I have a few dollars here in my pocket."

"How much?"

We start digging. "Well let's see—thirty, forty, sixty, eighty, a hundred, a hundred twenty dollars."

"That's fine. What else do you have?"

"Well, nothing. That's all."

"Where do you live?" He's still probing.

"In my house. Yes, I have a house."

"The house too, then." He writes that down.

"You mean I have to live in my camper?"

"You have a camper? That too. What else?"

"I'll have to sleep in my car."

"You have a car?"

"Two of them."

"Both become mine. Both cars. What else?"

"Well, you already have my money, my house, my camper, my cars, what more do you want?"

"Are you alone in this world?"

"No, I have a wife and two children...."

"Oh, yes, your wife and children too. What else?"

"I have nothing left! I'm left alone now."

Suddenly the seller exclaims, "Oh, I almost forgot! *You* yourself too! Everything becomes mine—wife, children, house, money, cars—and you too."

Then he goes on, "Now listen—I will allow you to use all these things for the time being. But don't forget that they are mine, just as you are. And whenever I need any of them, you must give them up, because now I am the owner."*

That's how it is when you're under the ownership of Jesus Christ.

---

*(*Disciple : A Handbook for New Believers* [Creation Press, 1995], 34, 35).

Have you heard of it?

Salvation is a gift, but it costs us everything. That's too big an order. That's too much for the carnal heart. And that leads us to the realization that this story about the woman at the well is a story about conversion—*conversion*. I am still angry about something. I'm going to remain angry until we find out more about the great theme of conversion. After thirty-six years of trying to talk about the gospel, I discover that we know nothing about conversion, the entire basis, the beginning point of the salvation experience. This is dishonoring. I went to my library. I have fifty-five volumes, big volumes of Charles Spurgeon sermons, every sermon he ever preached. I have volume after volume of the great preachers and the great preaching going back two thousand years to the early fathers. And the amount of material on conversion is comparatively nothing.

Well, you might say, the Bible doesn't say much about it. "The wind blows wherever it pleases" (John 3:8). We cannot understand the wind, neither can we understand this. We better try harder, neighbor. I want to know what it means. I want to be sure that I am converted, to know that the people I work with are converted, to know how to reach young people who need to be converted. I want to know what it means to be converted again tomorrow and the next day, until Jesus comes. There are big questions we ought to understand. Maybe for starters we can get into this story a little further.

The woman at the well had said in essence, "What was good enough for the fathers is good enough for us." That's an old argument, moth eaten. Then "Jesus answered, 'Everyone who drinks this water will be thirsty again, but whoever drinks the water I give him will never thirst. Indeed, the water I give him will become in him a spring of water welling up to eternal life' " (John 4:13, 14). At this point, in verse 15, the woman said to Him, " 'Sir, give me this water so that I won't get thirsty and have to keep coming here to draw water.' "

Notice the progression of her way of addressing Jesus through the story. First, she says, "How is it that you, a *Jew*, ask something of me, a Samaritan." Now she's getting a little more delicate. *"Sir,* give me of this water." And here we see the phenomenon of conversion taking place. The first step in conversion, or at least in coming to Christ, is a desire for something better, and Jesus is awakening this desire.

The woman had had this kind of desire for a long time. She had been looking for a better husband. She had five of them, and she was now with someone who was not her husband. This is not something that began and ended with the woman at the well. She had gotten tired of the vows and ceremonies and was going to make sure before another vow. She was not satisfied. And the water pot sitting on the edge of the well was simply a symbol of the fact that the systems of this world do not satisfy. It's all right to look for water, pure water. But if we are looking for what the water pot might have symbolized, it's an endless search. When she said, "Sir, give me this water," she was beginning to get the message.

She was beginning to realize that when you ask someone to give you something, you're admitting that you cannot produce it, you cannot earn it, you cannot deserve it, you can only ask for it. She's beginning to roll with what Jesus was teaching a whole nation, and the world ever since. It's a gift.

At this point Jesus said, " 'Go call your husband.' " Things got real quiet around there, and she got sweaty palms and began to prepare her side-step maneuver, because she was afraid that He would probe deeper. He did.

She said, "I have no husband."

Jesus said, "You're right. You have had five."

Then the woman said, in verse 19, " 'Sir, . . . I can see that you are a prophet.' " Here again we see the progression of the way she addresses Jesus, the conviction deepening that she is dealing with someone more than the average stranger. He is now a prophet. Then she comes in with her fancy footwork. "Which is the right church to go to?" That's what happens when you get nervous and the Holy Spirit is coming down hard on a hardened heart, because God is not pushy, but He is persistent. She said, "Let's talk about something concerning the history of our people."

The Samaritans were the product of intermarriage during the Babylonian captivity. They were a combination of Jew and "heathen," and they were at great enmity with the Jews. They had had rival temples, but the Samaritans had some disasters concerning their temple and it lay in ruins. They had rival holy mountains, and the question "Where should you go to church?" was a source of continuous discussion.

At this point, Jesus said something that is pertinent even to us today. He said, "It doesn't matter where you worship. It's how you worship that counts." Then He said these interesting words that were something of a prediction. "Yet a time is coming and has now come when the true worshipers will worship the Father in spirit and truth, for they are the kind of worshipers the Father seeks. God is spirit, and his worshipers must worship in spirit and in truth" (John 4:23, 24).

There is a big difference between being religious and being spiritual. There is a big difference between knowing the rules and regulations and standards and dogma of the church, and knowing God. God is a spirit. A mathematician once told me that God lives in another dimension. Well, I guess there's nothing new about that. And if we could see into the next dimension, as Elisha's servant did, then it would all become clear.

The other dimension in which God lives, along with the angels, in the heavenly city, which might be a fourth- or fifth-dimension city, is all the difference of night and day in terms of the spirit in which we live. The only person who can worship God in spirit as well as truth is the one who has become spiritual, and the only One who can affect that is God. The method by which it happens is something called conversion. We see this happening here by the well. It's happening with a one-soul audience. And it's exciting, because the same regard that Jesus had for that one soul, He still has for you today.

Do you have a desire for something better? I do. Do you have an understanding, even a little understanding of the knowledge of the plan of salvation, of the gospel? You do, and that's why you're reading this book and why you like to talk about these things. Do you understand that it is a gift that we cannot earn, that we cannot merit, that it comes only from God? His well is too deep for us, apart from His interventions. Will you join the woman at the well, realizing your sinfulness?

We're talking here about the classical sinner, in the classical way. But there is a worse kind of sinner. Conversion means to turn, or to turn around. There is a different kind of turning around than simply from our usual sins. It could be that for third- and fourth-generation church members, the turnaround is the turning from our own righteousness to His righteousness, and according to *Steps to Christ,* that is the most difficult battle of all. It is easy for God to reach sinners—harlots and thieves of the classical order. It is very difficult for God to reach proud people who have been doing just fine, thank you. "I wouldn't think of committing an immoral act. I'm a good man, God. Take care of the drunk in the gutter, and keep Your stars and planets from crashing into each other. But I'm a good person. I don't need You." That's the big one. Only the miracle of conversion can take us to that state where we turn from our own righteousness and our own goodness to the goodness of God, and that is the only kind of goodness there is.

At this point in the story we notice this woman coming to the point of surrender, because when Jesus talked about the spiritual things, the Holy Spirit took her the next step.

Jesus had said, "A time is coming and has now come when the true worshipers will worship the Father in spirit and *truth.*" My own subculture is good at talking about truth. You've heard of it: "Our grandparents came into the *truth* eighty years ago." "We found the *truth* in South Dakota." "I accepted the *truth.*" The truth without the Spirit is not worth a dime. God isn't looking primarily for people who know the truth about distinct points of doctrine. He is looking for people who know Him who is "the Truth and the Way and the Life." He is looking for people who demonstrate the truth by their love. God has a great deal of concern for those whom bad news about other people is the only good news for them. Ron Halverson said it well at camp meeting one summer, "The problem with the gospel is that it is good news. If it were bad news, we would have been happy to pass it on and the work would have been finished long ago." God is looking for people who see in this Stranger at the well someone they want to be like.

When Jesus got down to this point the woman said to Him, " 'I know that Messiah' " (called Christ) " 'is coming.' " Something is trying to resurrect itself in her memory. She has studied, in her quiet moments, the literature of her ancestors. And she knows about the Christ, the Messiah who is to come. She said, " 'I know that Messiah . . . is coming. When he comes, he will explain everything to us' " (John 4:25). And then Jesus did what He didn't do down at the temple in Jerusalem. He declared directly and simply, " 'I who speak to you am he.' " That's all it took. The woman at the well immediately left the well. She left her water pot (and that's not a bad idea; let's all leave our water pots), and she rushed to the city because she had something to tell.

It is interesting to notice about the genuine Christian witness, that no sooner does the person come to Christ, than there is born in his heart a desire to tell someone else what a precious Friend he has found in Jesus. Here she was in the presence of Someone who could tell her everything she did. (This is an overstatement; He really hadn't. He had only told her about one phase in her life. But it's like the lightning that strikes in the dark of night and hits only the oak tree, but everything else is illuminated at the same time.) She is impressed by this. She rushes to town, and she tells the men. Very interesting. The women had quit listening to her a long time ago. She tells the men, " 'Come, see a man who told me everything I ever did. Could this be the Christ?' " She moves from a *Jew* to *Sir* to *you're a prophet*, to *maybe the Messiah* and now *the Christ*.

Well, we're all impressed by the spectacular. If someone were to come along and tell us everything we ever did, we would be impressed too.

A group of students at La Sierra University several years ago got involved in charismatic worship, glossolalia, and the like in Los Angeles. Thirty or forty of them used to go into town, and some of them would come home "slain by the spirit," stiff as logs, carried by their friends. They were impressed because a complete stranger could sit down and tell them all about their lives and their problems and their sins in detail. They said, "This must be supernatural." And it was. But which spirit? Just because something supernatural happens doesn't mean that it's of God. And just because the stranger at the well can tell me everything I've ever done doesn't prove he is the Messiah. There were other proofs that thrilled the woman's heart, because there is something more important than being told everything you've ever done.

At the end of a thousand years and a little bit longer from now, people will stand in the presence of One who can tell them everything they ever did. Millions will be on the inside of a giant city with dimensions we cannot fathom, a multitude that no one can number; and millions will be on the outside from every generation. The people on the outside will stand there, as the audio-visual department comes on and that great screen high above God's throne shows the whole story from beginning to end. Everyone will see themselves in the picture. No one will move. On that day it will be a tragedy if we stand on the outside in the presence of One who knows everything we've ever done. It will be nothing but good news if we stand with Him and it's all covered by His blood. That was the case of the woman at the well. She not only met Someone who could tell her everything she ever did but was in the presence of Someone who loved her and was winning her to His kingdom.

She told them, "Come, see a man." The men followed her. Watch them as they come. She is streaking across the wheat fields toward the well again with these men following behind, for other reasons this time. They come into the presence of this One. Then something fantastic happens at the end of this story. "Many of the Samaritans from that town believed in him because of the woman's testimony, 'He told me everything I ever did'" (John 4:39). Verses 41 and 42 say, "And because of his words many more became believers. They said to the woman, 'We no longer believe just because of what you said; now we have heard for ourselves, and we know that this man really is the Savior of the world.'"

And that's the way it ended. Not only is He a Jew. Not only is He a kind sir. Not only is He a prophet. Not only is He the Messiah. Not only is He the Christ. He is the Savior of the world.

I'm thankful for the story from long ago that gives us hope today. I'm thankful we can be in the presence of Someone who knows us well, who still says, "Come drink of the water that I have to give." As we look wistfully toward heaven, may we have the solid assurance that God knows and accepts and understands. And may we join the woman at the well in witness to what the Lord has done for us.

OTHER BOOKS BY MORRIS VENDEN:

Nothing to Fear
Devotions intended to prepare Christians for the end times and to deliver them from unnecessary fear. In classic Venden style, this beloved author gives us daily food for thought on topics such as, "How to Be Ready," "Revival and Reformation," "The Shaking Time," "Latter Rain Preparation," "Wrestling with God," and 15 others.
0-8163-1695-3. Paperback. US$9.99, Can$14.99.

How Jesus Treated People
A look at how Jesus treated the many different types of people He encountered, with encouragement for us to follow His example.
0-8163-0621-4. Paperback. US$9.99, Can$14.99.

How to Know God's Will in Your Life
Learn how much weight you can give to the advice of others, how to understand what you find in God's Word, and how important your feelings are in the decision process.
0-8163-0719-9. Paperback. US$8.99, Can$13.49.

Modern Parables
Through the years, Pastor Venden has used parables to help bring heaven a little closer to earth. He's now compiled the best-loved parables from his many sermons into one book.
0-8163-1196-X. Paperback. US$10.99, Can$16.49.

Order from your ABC by calling **1-800-765-6955**, or get online and shop our virtual store at **www.AdventistBookCenter.com**.
• Read a chapter from your favorite book
• Order online
• Sign up for email notices on new products

Prices subject to change.